Experience is
Everything

Experience is
Everything

Winning Customers'
Hearts, Minds, and Wallets
in the Era of NOW CX

ENG TAN, DANIEL RODRIGUEZ
& THE FOLKS AT

First edition December 2021

ISBN 979-8-9852002-0-1 (hardcover)

ISBN 979-8-9852002-1-8 (eBook)

Published by Simplr Inc.

www.simplr.ai

TABLE OF CONTENTS

"A core focus of our effort is based on the recognition that our customers have varying needs, and one of their most important needs is to have choice."

Safra Catz
CEO, Oracle

"In a world where products and services are becoming more and more commoditized, customer experience is the only true differentiator."

Annette Franz
Founder and CEO, CX Journey

PART 1

The Stakes Have Been Raised: Serving the NOW Customer

CHAPTER 1

You're Neglecting Your Customers Without Even Knowing It

A Hidden Killer

Customer experience is in the midst of a crisis. An existential threat to businesses and brands. Although this threat is playing out in real time and in plain sight, it is largely invisible to a lot of people who work in customer service. Even more so to many C-suite leaders who aren't in touch with consumers every day. Interestingly enough, this crisis recalls another one that plagued the wine industry more than 150 years ago. We'll explain.

* * *

In 1863, wine growers in the French village of Pujaut were dismayed to see their cash crops literally withering on the vine. Vineyards that had produced robust harvests just one year prior were deteriorating right before their eyes. The death of a single grapevine would only

3

hint at the damage to follow, as disease gradually overtook nearby plants, then ultimately wiped out entire vineyards. Soon, the devastation spread across all of France and even spilled into other European countries, ultimately destroying more than 40% of grapevines in France alone, laying waste to countless wineries and siphoning an estimated 10 billion Francs from the French economy.[1]

For mid-nineteenth century winemakers, the crisis was clear. The cause was not. The sunlight, rainfall, and soil conditions hadn't changed. Prior to deteriorating, the plants themselves had shown no outward signs of pestilence, disease, or rot. With no inkling of what they were dealing with, growers were powerless to stop the spread.

It wasn't until 1868 that botanist Jules-Emile Planchon discovered the culprit: a near-microscopic, sapsucking insect that feeds on the roots of grapevines and gradually cuts off the flow of water and nutrients to the plants. Inspecting root specimens beneath his microscope's lens, Planchon remarked that while there was nothing visible to the naked eye, "Suddenly under the magnifying lens of the instrument appeared an insect, a plant louse of yellowish colour, tight on the wood, sucking the sap... it is not one, it is not ten, but hundreds, thousands... They are everywhere."[2]

The pest—known as *Phylloxera vastatrix*—was native to North America, where the rootstock of local vines had developed a defense system in the form of a sticky coating that both repelled the bugs and sealed bitten areas to prevent rot. But European vines had not evolved any natural defenses, and French vineyards soon became fertile feeding grounds for these non-indigenous invaders. Indeed, they *were* everywhere. And as the phylloxera did their dirty work, hidden deep in the soil, they spread silently for years, inflicting unprecedented damage across entire wine regions. And it all happened out of sight, beneath the feet of wine growers who were both unaware and unprepared.

You may be wondering how a North American bug found its

way to European shores in the mid-1800s. After all, Europeans had already been importing and experimenting with American vines in their soil for a few centuries by that point, and nothing like this had happened before. It just might be, as food and drink writer Chris Simms once noted in *New Scientist*, that the phylloxera's "arrival in France was the bitter fruit of technological progress." By the mid-nineteenth century, the advent of steamships had shortened the duration of Transatlantic travel to the point that phylloxera clinging to American vines could now, for the first time, survive the entire trip across the ocean.

You might also be curious about how viticulturalists brought an end to the Great French Wine Blight so that today we can still sip a nice Bordeaux and not just swig a Chateau Binghamton. As vineyard owners tried everything from coating plants in hot wax to burying live frogs beneath each root, two French wine growers— Leo Laliman and Gaston Bazille—landed on an innovative solution. By grafting American rootstock onto European vines, they created resilient next generation plants that were phylloxera-resistant below the soil yet retained the unique genetic composition of the grapes growing above ground. In essence, the French wine industry was saved by revitalizing an age-old approach with some newfound ingenuity and a deliberate act of evolution. And today, almost every wine growing region in the world uses American rootstock to successfully deter phylloxera (a truly global challenge) from destroying their vines.

Now, all of this begs the question: What does a root-munching pest from 150 years ago have to do with customer experience today? Well, you might be surprised.

You see, we believe that there is a similar blight harming many businesses today. One that has been unleashed by technological progress and calls for an innovative response. One that is happening right before our eyes, but that many organizations can't see for themselves. One that, left unchecked over time, can cause even your strongest customer relationships to whither on the vine.

At Simplr, we call this blight "customer neglect."

The Roots of Customer Neglect

When Amazon introduced their Prime Now same-day delivery service in the Boston metro, it blew our minds. More importantly, it raised our expectations for every single shopping experience we've had since. After humble beginnings in a smattering of New York City neighborhoods in 2014, Prime Now currently offers millions of people in major cities across America and around the world the speed and convenience of one- or two-hour delivery for everything from milk to mittens. Before experiencing this ourselves—clicking through thousands of available products and having our selections dropped on our doorsteps in less time than it takes to watch a feature film—both of us were more than satisfied with Amazon's basic Prime level of service. We would have been happy to pay an annual subscription fee for the miracle of fast, reliable two-day shipping. This in itself was already a vast improvement compared to the 7-10 business days (or more!) offered elsewhere on the internet. But now, *instant-on* and *always-on* have become the new standard by which millions of people just like us measure the quality of nearly every experience they have with just about any company.

Of course, speedy shipping isn't the entire point. It's speedy *everything*. Matt McCarron, vice president of operations at childcare products company Happiest Baby explains, "People don't just want to *receive* things right away. They want to start getting the benefits of the product right away too, getting what they expected *from* the product right off the bat. Speed needs to flow through the company from an efficient supply chain all the way through responsive and readily available service right when your customer needs it."

Now, if Amazon Prime Now's unimaginable speed, efficiency,

and ease of access were a unique case, even that might be enough to reshape consumer expectations across the board. But the fact is that there are a host of other innovative companies driving equally profound shifts in what buyers expect of brands.

Spotify and Netflix put a lifetime of on-demand entertainment at our fingertips, while even newer over-the-top (OTT) media services like Disney+, HBO Max, and Paramount Plus bring the newest movies to our homes the moment they're released. Instacart lets us stock our shelves from the comfort of our couch, providing doorstep delivery within hours of placing an order. DoorDash brings our favorite restaurant meals to our kitchen tables, often in thirty minutes or less. Uber provides private rides within minutes, at any time around the clock. Social networks trump news networks in reporting events as they happen live.

All of these examples speak to a game-changing shift toward a real-time economy that has been underway for more than a decade. As far back as 2010, digital transformation expert Greg Verdino advocated "doing business at the speed of now," writing that "the real-time Web demands that companies boot instantaneously in order to react to negative situations when they arise or capitalize on unexpected new business opportunities. Delays of a couple of days or even a few hours... mark the difference between failure and success."[3]

It should come as no surprise that the customer has changed. We've all changed. Today's customer expects instant access, immediate gratification, rapid resolutions, and engaged interactions from their brands, courtesy of the real-time economy and the higher-than-high standards set by companies like Amazon. Today's customer is always online—and always *on*—through chat, messaging, email, and social media.

They expect the same from you. As much as our fast-paced, hyper-connected, hyper-competitive world has created a new type of customer, it has also created a new covenant between companies and their customers. A covenant to engage each and every customer on their own terms. Yet too many companies still force customers to go where the business is set up to serve them, deflecting volume but not actually solving the customer's need here and now. Think about it: Are you pushing your customers away by limiting support to *your* business hours or *your* preferred channels? Are you relying on unhelpful bots, frustrating self-service tools or FAQs, essentially telling your online customers, "Figure it out yourself"?

The hard truth is this: Anything short of meeting this new consumer—think of them as the *NOW* Customer—right where they are amounts to nothing less than customer neglect. It's worse than a bad experience, although it *is* that; it's an experience that leaves the customer feeling dissatisfied, unimportant, angry, and disengaged. It's bad business.

In *Chapter 2*, we're going to take a closer look at just how bad this business can be, but first it's important to understand the NOW Customer, how they're different from the customers who have come before them, and why you might be neglecting them without even knowing it.

Meet the NOW Customer

Perhaps we've given you the impression that today's consumers are nothing more than a modern-day Veruca Salt from *Willy Wonka and the Chocolate Factory*—spoiled complainers, making unrealistic demands of everyone around them, belting out "I Want It Now" right up to the moment they topple into the trash heap. For better or worse, it's not so simple.

When it comes to customer service, immediacy is certainly an imperative. In their first post-COVID-19 *State of the Connected Customer* report, CRM giant Salesforce.com found that "83% of customers expect to engage with someone immediately when contacting a company—up from 78% in 2019."[4] And it's no surprise that, at a time when consumers spend more time online than off, they are increasingly likely to interact with companies through digital channels and expect to do more online shopping than they've ever done before. "88% of customers expect companies to accelerate their digital initiatives" post-pandemic and more than half expect companies to expand their methods of customer engagement to include more digital touchpoints.[5] This is particularly notable given that the average consumer already uses nine channels to browse inventory, seek service, and make purchases[6]—and expects a fast, consistent, contextually-relevant experience across all of them.

This begs the question: *how fast is fast enough?* Well, the brands that scored highest for CX in our own 2021 study of 800 online retailers answered emails in less than 15 minutes and responded to live chats in under 30 seconds.[7] If that sounds like a tall order, even during your regular business day, consider that peak online browsing hours (generally, 5pm to midnight Eastern time) often begin after your best rep has logged off for the night.

It's clear that meeting the NOW Customer in the moment puts the onus on your organization to be omni-channel, instant-on, and always-on. But there's more to the NOW Customer than the mere need for speed.

A company's ability to make a human connection matters an awful lot to consumers in the NOW era. A full 68% of customers expect brands to demonstrate empathy (even though they say only 38% actually do so consistently). More than 80% say a company's trustworthiness matters more than it did a year ago (although more than a third question whether companies truly have their customers' best interests in mind). And ethics, transparency, and corporate accountability are more likely to shape both brand perceptions and purchase behaviors in the post-COVID-19 era.[8] Ultimately, "53% of customers say they feel an emotional connection to the brands they buy the most," and these loyal customers have a 306% higher lifetime value and will recommend the brands they love 26% more than the average.[9]

Speed. Availability. Empathy. Trust. Ethics. Transparency. Accountability. Let's be honest with ourselves: These are not the NOW Customer's unreasonable aspirations. They are *any* person's reasonable expectations. And they are the basic building blocks of a NOW-era customer experience—the kind of experience that can be a powerful differentiator at a time when 80% of people say the experience a company provides is as important as its products and services. The kind of positive customer service experience that leads 91% of buyers to make a repeat purchase and 78% to forgive a company even after it makes a mistake.[10]

Of course, just because these things are reasonable, that doesn't mean they're easy. Certainly not when NOW Customers are comparing the quality of your experience to the very best from any business. As customer experience expert Dan Gingiss says, "Most companies must realize that they are no longer competing against the guy down the street or the brand that sells similar products. Instead, they're competing with every other experience a customer has." In fact, our own research shows that 63% of shoppers base their customer service expectations on the best experiences they've ever had.[11] According to one study by marketing agency Wunderman Thompson, 75% of shoppers are actively comparing you with Amazon itself and wishing that you "offered the same level of service."[12]

It's a high bar, and if you fail to clear it, you'll make NOW Customers feel like neglected customers. And this is where things get stickier than vine sap.

The Neglect You Don't Expect

Clearly, no business sets out to neglect customers. But because of the ways in which the world has changed since the start of the digital revolution, the type of customer experience that served consumers (and companies) so well in the past have now become the root cause of a rampant customer neglect problem.

Before we go deeper, let's define what we mean by customer neglect. Put simply, customer neglect happens when an actual or would-be buyer is actively—or inadvertently—ignored by the people who work at the business with which they're trying to engage. In a brick-and-mortar retail setting, this would involve not answering an in-person customer's questions, not answering the phone, or putting callers on hold for an eternity.

Today, customer neglect has become much more nuanced. Your shopper is still being ignored, but it's happening across a much wider (and more complicated) spectrum of touch points: delayed email responses, lack of live chat, unanswered social media direct messages, long hold times, full voicemail boxes, unresolved Yelp reviews, and so on. Regardless of the form customer neglect takes, one thing is painfully clear. *It costs companies business.*

In a recent Simplr survey, we found that one-third of consumers feel that they have been ignored or left hanging by an online retailer. Additionally, 51% of customers will never do business with a company again after just one negative experience.[13]

So yes, customer neglect is a big—and very real—problem for a lot of companies. Still, maybe you think that it isn't an issue for *your* company. You may point to your good-to-very-good Customer Satisfaction (CSAT) ratings and Net Promoter Scores (NPS). But those metrics don't tell the whole story. In fact, for every customer who gives you an NPS rating (good, bad, or otherwise), 10 other customers tell you nothing.[14] *Nada.* That's 10 people who had an experience with your brand, but you have no idea whether they loved it, hated it, or really didn't care either way.

At least you know where your "not likely to recommend" detractors stand. The *couldn't-be-bothered-to-respond* customers are a total unknown to you, a breeding ground for hidden neglect. In fact, we believe that there are seven forms of customer neglect. You may only be aware of three of them—and you may not even realize that one of those is a problem. The rest are lurking beneath the surface, eating away at your profitability and brand equity without your knowledge. Let's take a quick look at all seven ways customer neglect manifests in the form of seven types of neglected customers.

The Seven Types of Neglected Customers

Most businesses will have no trouble recognizing the first two types of neglected customers, as both live "above the surface" and don't hesitate to make themselves known to your conventional or digital support teams.

The Vocal Complainer

The first type of neglected customer feels disappointed in or frustrated by your brand and isn't shy about letting you know. Whether they felt cast adrift without enough information about their order, waited too long for a customer service response, or got left hanging without a satisfactory answer to their question, this customer is going to let you know they're unhappy. They'll complain to your customer service reps, ask to speak to a manager, send an angry email or vent their frustration on live chat. In *Hug Your Haters*, marketing expert Jay Baer called these complainers "offstage haters" because they tend to stick to legacy channels where the likelihood of a response is highest albeit not nearly high enough. Offstage haters may not care if anyone else finds out, as long as they get satisfaction.

The Social Media Megaphone

This customer makes their neglect known in a big way by berating your brand on social media. Having learned a few tricks from nearly two decades' worth of big brand social media fails, *Megaphones* take their grievances to networks like Facebook, Twitter, Instagram, or

Seven Types of Neglected Customers

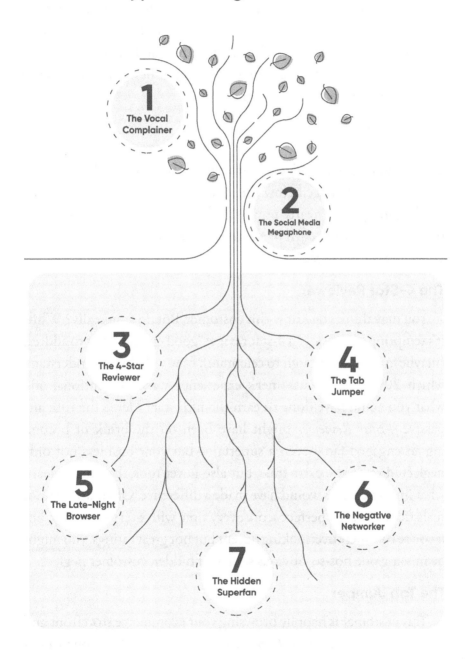

Snapchat, putting your brand on blast on the most public forum they can find. To Jay Baer, these are "onstage haters" who are often so disappointed by a neglectful interaction in traditional channels that they turn to social media, online review sites, and discussion boards where they want more than a mere solution—they want an audience to share in their righteous indignation.

* * *

The remaining five neglected customer types are a different story. They do their damage below the surface in ways that make it more challenging (if not nearly impossible) for your company to reverse the rot, given your current customer service model and the way you're measuring success.

The 4-Star Reviewer

You may think you know this customer. But do you, really? While it's tempting to consider a 4-star review "good enough" not to address (maybe even good enough to celebrate), how well do you understand which 20% of that customer's experience wasn't exceptional and what you could have done to earn the fifth star? Here's the rub: any passive *4-Star Reviewer* might have been on the brink of becoming an engaged fan—even a superfan—but your business not only neglected to go the extra mile, but also never took the time to learn what improvements would have made a difference. Obviously, it's not realistic to expect a perfect score every time with every customer, but if you're routinely overlooking decent but not great ratings, you might be missing one not-so-obvious source of hidden customer neglect.

The Tab Jumper

This customer is happily browsing your ecommerce storefront and they're ready to buy now. *Great news!* Except that they don't care if it's from you or a one-click-away competitor. If you're not available and able to answer questions quickly at the very moment this buyer is making their decision, they're likely to jump to another tab and complete their purchase from someone else's site. If your online experience is too cumbersome or demands too much effort on the part of the customer, they'll jump to another brand faster than you can say *click*.

The Late-Night Browser

If you stop serving customers before they're done shopping for the day, you can miss out on key browsing (and buying) times. We know that ecommerce primetime starts after business hours end and can extend well into the night. Late-Night Browsers hit your site or mobile app and, failing to find what they're looking for or any way to engage with your company in real-time, leave before you ever knew they were there. By the time your team is back on the clock, they've purchased from another seller.

The Negative Networker

This customer is one of the toughest to detect. They had a bad experience, but never contacted the company through legacy channels, left a negative review or lambasted it on social media. They may lurk among the 10 out of every 11 people who never let your company know what it was like doing business with your brand, but they'll have no problem letting 15 or so of their friends and family know just how dissatisfied they were.[15] Their weapon of choice is traditional, offline word-of-mouth.

The Hidden Superfan

This neglected customer actually loves your brand, but are you loving them back? This customer may not be a vocal reviewer, take to social media to share their love, or make the time to complete your CSAT survey—but they're the kind of quiet customer who would choose you over your competition every time. If only you weren't neglecting to recognize, engage, and reward them for their budding brand fandom. Sure, you may not have *lost* much by neglecting this customer, but you could be missing big opportunities to cultivate more brand loyalty and capture more revenue. The kicker: Because this customer is already primed to be a superfan, catching the upside wouldn't have required all that much extra effort.

* * *

As you can see, there are lots of ways neglect can manifest for NOW Customers—and that's dangerous for your brand. As a CX professional, you have to be positioned to detect and solve customer neglect issues before they have a chance to harm your business. So...

What's Holding You Back?

Let's be clear about something: None of this is your fault. As a committed CX professional who understands that experience is indeed everything, you are an important part of the solution. With that out of the way, though, the question remains: Why hasn't your organization already eradicated customer neglect?

We believe three main things are holding you back. First, the traditional contact center model that you've inherited is not well adapted to the NOW Customer era. Second, the way our industry measures success misses the telltale signs of neglect and fails to account for the real value of a high-quality customer experience: increased revenue. Third, as much as *you* believe in the power of CX, odds are that your organization isn't (yet) treating customer service as the strategic imperative it needs to be.

Over the course of this book, we'll cast a critical eye on these challenges. But more importantly, we'll chart the path forward by showing you exactly what your organization needs to do to perfectly align your CX with the needs of today's most demanding and connected customers. To deliver an experience every bit as excellent as the best experiences offered by any company, anywhere. To make experience *everything*. To win the hearts, minds, and wallets of your NOW Customers.

Step Into the NOW

In other words, we'll help you see how your organization can enter the era of NOW CX—by adopting a radically different approach to people, technology, and intelligence inside your customer service organization so that you can deliver the kind of instant-on, always-on, omni-channel engagement your NOW Customers crave. Eradicate customer neglect. Treat every customer like a VIP. Uncover new opportunities for accelerating the first sale and re-engaging, cross-selling, and upselling customers at every touchpoint throughout the customer lifecycle.

A NOW experience is a *wow* experience. And at a time when most companies are trapped in the land of status quo CX, it's a powerful way to differentiate your business from the competition and become an undisputed leader in customer experience.

Needless to say, we think this is big. *How big?* Well, that's the $75 billion question that we'll tackle in the next chapter.

CHAPTER 2

How Much Is Customer Neglect Costing You?

The $75 Billion Problem

In their most recent *Serial Switchers* study, NewVoiceMedia estimated that U.S. companies are losing $75 billion per year as a result of bad customer experiences.[1] Needless to say, a bad experience is bad for business, but it might be difficult to wrap your head around a number so large that it boggles the mind. So, let's make the cost of neglect a bit more tangible by looking at a well-known, real-world example before turning our attention to one way you can get a handle on the financial fallout from neglect in your own organization.

Peloton's Pandemic Position

Picture this: It's mid-2020, in the early days of social distancing, and people everywhere are adjusting to a new lifestyle where home has become not only where the heart is, but where the work, school, gym, and *everything* are.

As the COVID-19 pandemic took hold of our "old" way of life, many businesses and entire industries struggled. Think: brick-and-mortar retail, hospitality, air travel, and education, along with many other sectors that rely on a safe environment for in-person interactions. At the same time, companies that hinge on digital or home-based experiences saw a social distance silver lining grow their businesses faster than ever. Peloton was one of these companies.

With its high-end home fitness equipment and streaming classes, Peloton was in an enviable position in 2020 as fitness-focused consumers looked for ways to create the gym experience at home. Orders for Peloton's bikes and treadmills came in fast, but unfortunately, many customers ended up furious.

Supply, Demand, and Neglect

Supply chain issues—which affected many businesses the world over throughout 2020—created major shipping delays for Peloton and the NOW Customers eagerly awaiting their new fitness gear. But shipping delays on their own do not necessarily equate to neglect; it's about whether or not a company's customer experience team goes the extra mile to offer customers clarity and communication during the delay. Unfortunately in Peloton's case, the company was not positioned to assuage customer's concerns and connect on a human level during the height of the pandemic-fueled delays, precisely when a heightened sense of empathy was in high demand.

In fact, even as sales went through the roof, Peloton's stock price faltered in late 2020, and according to *MarketWatch*, customer experience challenges were at the center of the stock price dip Peloton (NASDAQ: PTON) was facing. "The fast growth is causing issues for the company as it attempts to field and fulfill orders, however, which may have contributed to a decline in Peloton stock."[2]

In a November 2020 letter to shareholders, Peloton addressed the company's unintended challenges with customer neglect:

"[Peloton's new product releases and fast growth] drove call volumes and unacceptably long wait times, well beyond our expectations, to reach our sales and support teams, which impacted our customer experience... Also, as we rapidly scale our organization to meet the extraordinary demand for our products, we realize that some of our members have faced extended delays associated with receiving our products or having support requests fulfilled."[3]

"Like An 'F You'"

A January 2021 *New York Times* piece titled 'Peloton's Rapid Rise Is Threatened by Its Slow Delivery' discussed the company's customer neglect problem: "Some customers have reported getting automated emails pushing their delivery dates out by a month or more, and then receiving little clarity from customer service representatives, who sometimes blame Peloton's shipping partners."[4]

In February 2021, several neglected Peloton buyers spoke to consumer technology website *The Verge* for an article about the fitness company's shipping issues and customer experience let-downs. One of the customers profiled was a woman who originally ordered a Peloton bike with her husband in November 2020, under the assumption that the couple would have their bike in time for Christmas. But the holiday came and went with no bike:

"Five days before the set delivery date, Peloton emailed the couple a generic message to say they'd have to keep waiting. The bike had been delayed by seven more weeks. The company hasn't offered them a discount or even a thorough explanation for a delay. 'For the amount of money you're spending,' [the customer] says, 'the delay felt like an F you.' In Peloton's lightning in a bottle of a year, it hasn't been able to keep up with demand, and customers are angry."[5]

Now, as fans of the brand ourselves, we feel it's only right to point out that Peloton likely never intended nor wanted anyone to feel neglected. But in the year when everything was rightfully labeled "unprecedented," that's exactly what happened.

Neglected Customers Streaming In

At the height of the company's pandemic-era shipping issues, Peloton's neglectful customer service approach resulted in many consumers feeling like they were left in the dark and that they were simply not valued by the company. And as neglect reared its ugly head, several of the neglected customer types we identified in *Chapter 1* were making their dissatisfaction known and taking their money to competing fitness brands. A few examples spring—or pedal—to mind:

The Vocal Complainer

Peloton has had to contend with unhappy customers reaching out through traditional customer service channels, leaving less than stellar reviews, and driving down the company's Better Business Bureau (BBB) rating to less than 1.5 out of 5.[6] Lively discussions also sprang up on a website called PelotonForum.com, with neglected customers venting their frustrations in public threads with titles like "Waiting six months for the bike +" and "Delivery and Customer Service EPIC FAIL."[7]

The Social Media Megaphone

During the pandemic perhaps more than ever, social media has provided customers with a favorite set of channels for airing grievances and making their neglect known. In Peloton's case, according to *The Verge*:

"Reports of months-long delays are spilling out onto social media, inundating Twitter and Peloton's official Facebook group with complaints. Other customers are taking to Peloton's Instagram comments to vent. 'Canceled our bike due to long delays,' one person wrote. 'Would not recommend Peloton. Bad customer service, and constant shipping delays.'"[8]

The Tab Jumper

Clearly, a $2,000+ home fitness bike is not a casual purchase for most, and the strength of the Peloton brand alone should have insulated the company from being shopped like a commodity. Despite these facts, Peloton still experienced a version of tab jumping from customers who got fed up and canceled orders altogether. In some cases, those customers switched over to a competing bike company or alternative fitness equipment brand in the hopes that they would get a similar product without the baggage of a bad experience.

The Negative Networker

For every one of the dissatisfied Peloton customers profiled in articles about the company's shipping and CX woes, we've got to assume there were many more quietly sharing their opinions and experiences with friends and family. When we polled the Simplr team to ask if anyone had ever heard from a friend about a negative experience with Peloton, several of our colleagues said yes. Even with our admittedly un-scientific poll, we found that members of our team had heard under-the-radar complaints that could have influenced others not to buy.

The Hidden Superfan

Now, some of you reading this chapter might be thinking, "Excuse me, I *love* my Peloton! I've never had a single issue!" Pandemic-era CX challenges aside, Peloton has built an enthusiastic customer base made up of countless superfans. When they found themselves in the thick of the shipping delay issue, could Peloton have connected with and activated Hidden Superfans to help show neglected customers another side of the "Pelo" experience? We're guessing yes. But did they? Not that we know of—a common misstep among brands that are so suddenly swept into a neglect nightmare is that they fail to recognize the importance of activating advocates who can amplify a competing, overwhelmingly positive counter-narrative that protects brand (and business) value, even in the face of a customer experience faux pas.

A $100+ Million Customer Neglect Price Tag

Repairing Peloton's customer neglect problem has come with a hefty price tag. In a company blog post, Peloton Co-Founder and CEO John Foley wrote:

> "We are investing over $100 million to help expedite the movement of Bikes and Treads globally, in order to meet our delivery commitments. On average, in the coming months, we will be incurring a transportation and delivery cost that is over ten times our usual cost per Bike and Tread, including, in many cases, shipping them by air instead of by sea. We are making this investment because we are as frustrated as you are that you don't have your Peloton Bike or Tread yet."[9]

Yes, that's $100 million to address supply chain problems, shipping problems, and delivery costs that are growing exponentially more expensive for the company. Additionally, the *Wall Street Journal* reported in February 2021 that the company had cut back on marketing efforts and doubled the size of its customer service operation to address long wait times and delivery cancellations that have angered many would-be customers.[10] Even more costs to bear, although we'd note that scaling up its support operation as a means to correct neglect and mitigate further CX challenges is a smart move.

Then there's the long-term view and potential future revenue loss that could stem from 2020's customer neglect issues. As global supply chain publication *Freight Waves* outlined, Peloton executives "understand the brand they have built and know the value of each customer lost is enormous... The company estimates its [lifetime value] to be $3,500/customer, but that is solely based on content subscriptions and is severely understated because Peloton customers, like Apple users, are likely to upgrade their hardware over the years."[11]

Ultimately, calculating the total cost of customer neglect is not a simple formula because there are so many factors at play. However, we can see in Peloton's case that the price tag is well north of $100 million when we consider what the company had to invest to solve supply chain issues and expand its customer service capabilities, the increased costs of transportation and delivery, and the lost customers who canceled orders or were influenced by others not to buy.

Customer Neglect is a Cost You Can't Afford

Of course, Peloton has lived to sweat another day, but there's no denying that it has been an expensive ride. Even after investing so much to address the initial issue, the company spent most of 2021 pedaling backwards, suffering from poor earnings and a falling stock price, while giving fast-following competitors more than enough runway to gain even more traction in the wake of these troubles.

We hate to have to say this, but a hard truth we've got to face is that not every company could withstand such a widespread and public customer neglect problem. And it can creep up more easily than you might think. Seemingly small CX infractions can add up quickly, and since NOW Customers are always on and super-connected, you can't afford to neglect them in any CX channel or at any time of day.

According to 2016 research from Forrester, 53% of customers are very likely to abandon a purchase if they don't get a quick answer for their question.[12] So, if you are neglecting customers when they're prepared to buy, roughly half will abandon you right off the bat. The opportunity was lost before you even realized the would-be customer was there.

Similarly, Zendesk reports that 50% of customers will find another customer service channel if they don't get a response within an hour.[13] And we'd add that consumer patience tends to have vastly different time spans depending on the customer service channel. You might be able to get away with an hour-long wait on email, but your customer would be long gone if you gave them the same delay on chat. So, if you have a neglect problem in your CX operation, you're likely to lose half of your buyers right off the bat. Then, as the other half (the half who didn't abandon right away) hop to other channels seeking a response, a poorly tuned omni-channel CX program could put those relationships at risk. Simply put, neglect on one channel could lead to neglect on another channel. And this adds to the customer's frustration—which will only add to *your* frustration in the long run.

Research Shows That Neglect Is a Costly Problem

In late 2020, Simplr commissioned a consumer study to understand shoppers' expectations, attitudes, and behaviors related to the upcoming holiday season. As part of this study, we also wanted to explore the concept of customer neglect, and we ended up with some interesting (and worrying) findings:[14]

- Of the 750 consumers who participated in that study, one-third reported having been left hanging or ignored by an online retailer's customer service, while 10% said they weren't sure. What this tells us is that too many companies are letting poor CX lead to experiences of customer neglect.
- Half of respondents said they were likely to tell a friend or post social media about a poor customer service experience,

and 55% said they are likely to leave a negative review of a retailer based on poor customer service. What this tells us is that consumers aren't very forgiving of brands and retailers' CX transgressions, and they are more likely than not to make their frustrations known.

- Four in 10 respondents reported that they have decided to stop shopping with a brand or retailer altogether because of a poor customer service experience. What this tells us is that the "silent killer" of customer neglect is absolutely affecting companies' revenue and customer lifetime value metrics.

As we were gathering consumer insights, Simplr also partnered with research firm Sinclair Metrics to conduct a "mystery shop" study over the Black Friday-Cyber Monday period in 2020. During those five frenzied days that kick off the holiday season, we sent a group of mystery shoppers to the websites of 652 ecommerce and retail companies where they engaged in 1,950 pre-sale customer service interactions across the two most commonly used digital CX channels: email and chat.

Based on the levels of customer neglect our research detected— stemming from issues ranging from delayed and nonexistent email responses to unhelpful and unavailable chats—we arrived at a finding that stunned us. Based on the results from that mystery shop study, crossed with SimilarWeb Pro insights and data from Simplr's customer service platform, we were able to estimate that many companies are missing out on up to $20 million per year due to customer neglect.[15] So, could *your* company be leaving up to $20 million on the table each year due to challenges that can be traced to *your* department? Let's see.

Calculating the Cost of Neglect

How can you know the cost of customer neglect at your company? Unfortunately, it isn't as simple to calculate as an easy 1, 2, 3. But we have developed a formula for estimating lost revenue due to customer neglect in the chat channel specifically, and you can use this to run different scenarios that make sense for your business. Here's how it works:

In Step 1, you take your average monthly website visitors and multiply that number by 0.75%, which is the average rate at which we see website visitors engaging with customer service chat. If you know your company's *actual* visitor-to-chatter rate, feel free to swap that number in the place of the 0.0075 for a more accurate assessment. The result you get in Step 1 is your average monthly chat-seeking customers.

In Step 2, you multiply the result you got in Step 1 by 63%, which is the average percentage of neglected chat-seekers according to our research chats (for example, when chats are too slow, when resolutions are unsatisfactory to customers, or when a company doesn't offer chat at all at a time when the buyer is shopping). Again, if you know your company's rate for unsuccessful chat engagement to be different, feel free to swap that number in the place of the 0.63.

The result you get in Step 2 is your monthly average number of neglected chat-seekers.

In Step 3, you take the result you got in Step 2 and multiply by your average purchase price. The result you get in Step 3 is your total estimated monthly cost of customer neglect in the chat channel alone.

To make this feel more tangible, let's run a few potential scenarios that use site traffic figures that vary from relatively low to somewhat substantial, and average purchase amounts that range from a modest purchase to a higher total cart.

Scenario 1: Low Traffic, Mid-Sized Purchase

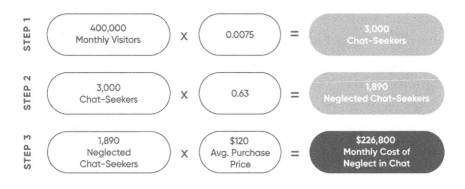

Scenario 2: High Traffic, Small Purchase

Scenario 3: Moderate Traffic, Large Ticket Purchase

As you can see, customer neglect has a real, relevant cost for any ecommerce company or traditional retailer with a digital presence. And it's important to keep in mind that this formula and any of these scenarios looks at lost revenue *per month* due to neglect in the chat channel *only*. Once you project the numbers out over the course of a full year and start factoring in neglect across every touchpoint throughout your customer service operation, the numbers can get pretty scary. But the numbers that really count are the numbers you've calculated for your own organization. Were they surprising, even scary, to you?

Frightened by Neglect? Keep Reading

We hope that you can see just how easy it can be for the financial impact of customer neglect in one situation, in one channel, and over the course of just one month to spiral into the industry-wide $75 billion problem we introduced at the start of this chapter. And we trust that, regardless of what your own calculations show, you'd agree that any dollar left on the table is one dollar more than you'd like to leave behind.

Now, between parasitic bugs and billions in lost revenue, this book might seem like it's shaping up to be a real downer. But that's all about to change. You didn't *really* think we'd leave you in a cold sweat without offering a solution to the customer neglect problem, did you? Let's turn the page (literally and figuratively) to learn how customer experience leaders like you can eradicate neglect with NOW CX.

CHAPTER 3

The NOW CX Approach Is the Only Way to Win

What the World Needs Now (Is NOW CX)

Customer experience is in the crosshairs of change. So far, we've shown that the world has entered the on-demand NOW era. All consumers are NOW Customers who browse, shop, and interact with brands and retailers on their own terms and timeline. The NOW Customer expects brands to respond to their needs instantly and with a personal touch, regardless of channel or time of day. When companies fail (or even struggle) to meet these expectations, their customers feel neglected—a substantial challenge that can cost those companies millions (even billions) but will often go undetected (and unaddressed) until it's almost too late to solve.

So, what are you doing about all this? The unfortunate truth is that most organizations are barely getting by, trying to make the best of an outmoded customer experience model that simply was not made for this modern era, your modern customers, and their modern demands. The system within which you're forced to work is, simply put, not up to the task.

The time is (*ahem*) now to move beyond the legacy contact center model—a model that was built for the analog era and is saddled with more baggage than a pack mule—and enter the era of NOW CX. Are you ready to join the movement?

Yes! But What Exactly is NOW CX?

This is a good time to define exactly what we mean when we say NOW CX, explain how it's different from the way you may be doing things today, highlight the advantages it offers over the legacy contact center model, and outline the key elements of a successful NOW CX strategy.

*   *   *

NOW CX is a new and different approach to exceeding the needs of the NOW Customer by empowering your organization to eradicate neglect, convert shoppers into buyers, and turn every customer into a five-star fan. The NOW CX model intelligently blends the best of humans and technology, enabling brands to give consumers an always-on, always-personal experience, whenever and wherever they want to engage.

*   *   *

Obviously though, there's more to it than that. Making the leap to NOW CX requires customer experience organizations to break free of five age-old constraints of the traditional contact center model. These constraints—and the strategic shifts you'll make as you break them—are:

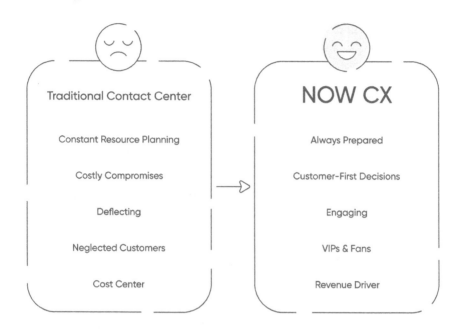

Let's look at each of these in more detail.

From Constant Resource Planning to Knowing You're Always Prepared

CX workforce planning is a never-ending grind. Forecasting is an imperfect science at best. You work hard trying to predict the unpredictable and lock in just the right level of staffing in the face of variable demand. You staff up (if you can) and invest the time, energy, and money necessary to train the team—all while struggling to stem sky-high agent attrition rates. And still, you get it wrong more than you get it right. It's frustrating. Your company and your customers deserve better. So do you.

Instead, what if you could always be ready for whatever comes next—without the constant planning, preparation and (frankly) guesswork that this would require in today's outdated contact center staffing model?

The NOW CX model means that you and your team are always prepared, without the arduous planning and often less-than-accurate forecasting you do today. You'll have peace of mind in knowing that you're ready for even the most sudden of spikes in volume without worrying about overstaffing, wasted budget, or less than perfect agent efficiency—and that you will finally be able to give your NOW Customers everything they demand and deserve.

From Making Costly Compromises to Making Customer-First Decisions

A contact center model based on fixed resources, scheduled shifts, and rigidity is out of sync with a world that demands flexibility, scalability, and an always-on change-readiness. This puts CX leaders in a tough spot—forced to make trade-offs that may save the company money but can cost more in lost customer loyalty and missed revenue opportunities. You pull levers, apply Band-Aids™, and make every compromise you can, all to provide a good-enough experience to customers who don't believe good enough is good enough.

But what if you didn't have to choose between what's right for your customer and what's right for your budget? What if you didn't need to make compromises that could cost you customers?

NOW CX aims to be truly compromise-free. It offers you the best of both worlds. Finally, you can truly put your customers first. You can choose what's best for them—engagement plus empathy, responsiveness plus relationship-build, and a VIP experience—without blowing your budget or breaking the bank. In fact, you can do this without *just* controlling your costs. You can actually grow your top line through excellent experience. For companies that get this right, "customer-first" is no longer just a slogan; it's their reality.

From Deflecting Volume to Engaging Everyone

Too many companies force customers to go where they can service them, deflecting volume but not actually solving the customer's need "here and now." But as we've already laid out, this is exactly the kind of thing that causes neglect and drives your NOW Customers to take their business elsewhere (and complain about your company while they do it).

Are you pushing your customers away by limiting support to your business hours or your preferred channels? Are you relying too heavily on automation—chatbots, FAQs, and other self-service options—essentially telling your customers to "figure it out yourself"?

When you do this (any of it or all of it), you put the burden on the customer to engage with you on *your* terms. As we've seen, the NOW Customer demands that you engage with them on their terms—whenever, wherever, and however they wish across an increasingly complex ecosystem of traditional and digital points of engagement. Failure to do so creates a profound disconnect between your company and its customers. The problem though, is that the legacy contact center model makes it difficult—if not impossible—to meet your customers where they are, consistently, efficiently, and at all hours of the day.

The NOW CX approach is as digital-by-default as your most demanding buyers. It's designed from the ground up as an always-on, instant-on, omni-channel engagement model for next level customer care. Whereas deflecting is neglecting, engaging proves that you're there for your customers and that you truly care about them and the experience they have with your company.

From Neglecting Customers to Creating VIPs & Fans

In *Chapter 1*, we dove deep into the topic of customer neglect, highlighting ways in which neglect proliferates among customers, causing revenue and reputational damage before a brand even realizes what's happening. Whether or not you realize that you have a neglect problem at your own company, you certainly know what customer neglect feels like, because you're not just a CX leader at your own company; You're another company's customer. Neglect is how you feel when you wait hours or even days for an email response. It's how you feel when a company's office hours don't jive with your "off" hours issue. It's how you feel when you're 10-minutes into a conversation with a bot that does little more than return scripted replies. You feel frustrated. You feel angry. You feel neglected.

It's bad at an individual level. But because you *are* a CX leader, poor service isn't just personal. It's professional. No matter how well-intentioned you may be, the legacy contact center model is built around a set of constraints that practically guarantee backlogs, wait times, sluggish response rates, and limited availability. Waiting makes a customer feel neglected. Rapid response plus a top-notch resolution to a burning issue makes the customer feel like they matter to your business. That's what creates a VIP experience and turns a customer into a five-star fan. And that's exactly what NOW CX is designed to do.

From Managing CX as a Cost Center to Making CX a Revenue Driver

Legal, accounting, HR, IT, facilities management, the company cafeteria—all cost centers. But Customer Experience? The only function in the entire organization that is routinely and regularly in direct contact with the people who actually keep your company in business—that's a cost center too? Well, it's probably because company leadership sees CX as a support function, a reactive contact center of firefighters dealing with problems, handling complaints, and addressing dissatisfaction before it burns out of control.

The truth is that every connection with any customer is a revenue opportunity—whether you're streamlining a sale to a first-time buyer, identifying opportunities for upsell and cross-sell, nurturing a relationship with a repeat customer, or appeasing an unhappy buyer to prevent churn. So, you're not firefighters. You're revenue igniters. When your organization sees customer experience not as a cost center but as a revenue generator, you'll earn the opportunity to design and invest in a model to make sure your CX team can ignite every opportunity (not just douse every challenge)—and you'll position CX as an engine for growth.

Of the five shifts that differentiate NOW CX from the legacy contact center model, we consider this one to be the most profound. Once achieved, it truly gives customer experience leaders a seat at the table and makes CX a vital driver of company-wide strategy.

How NOW?

By this point, the advantages of a NOW CX approach over the legacy contact center should be clear enough. So, you're probably asking yourself how your organization can make turn theory into practice. What does it take to make NOW CX a reality?

A new approach to three things, actually: people, technology, and intelligence.

First, you'll need to rethink your approach to people. NOW CX requires a flexible, scalable customer experience workforce, on-tap to provide your customers with efficient, empathetic service and support at all times and on every digital channel where NOW consumers want to interact. Done right, NOW CX makes overstaffing and understaffing, over-investing and cutting corners, and even the painful process of forecasting in the face of the unknown become things of the past.

In *Part 2* of this book, we will take a critical look at why the fixed-resource contact center model is such a problem and propose a bold solution that leverages a "human cloud" to maximize flexibility and scalability. We will explore how CX can tap into an on-demand workforce that is always-on and instant-on with no downtime, outages, or waste. We will show how brands can benefit when they shift from traditional contact center staffing to a distributed network of modern CX specialists who have work-from-anywhere independence and other benefits that result in higher agent satisfaction and engagement that—in turn—result in the kind of customer satisfaction and engagement that turns your buyers into fans.

Second, you'll need the right technology. You'll need unified and connected technology that enables your customer experience team to deliver a consistent, high caliber experience across all customer touch points, with minimal context-switching, more productivity, and greater speed. You'll need technologies that help your agents ramp quickly and with less training time without sacrificing quality or on-brand performance.

Technology is already your second largest budget line item after people. And most customer service organizations are already investing in chatbots and other forms of automation to facilitate customer self-service and improve agent productivity. This is all a great start, but we believe that the right technology can do so much more. Imagine, for example, employing a powerful artificial intelligence platform that is 'trained' with company data, empowers agents to ramp faster to deliver in-the-moment capacity at-scale, and provides in-context guidance and decision flows that result in on-brand interactions and satisfactory resolutions. Imagine technology that truly empowers your people while delivering real value for your purchasers. Technologies like these are a recurring theme throughout *Parts 2* and *3*; As you'll see in *Part 4*, technology adoption is an important measure of your organization's NOW CX maturity.

And third, you'll need more actionable intelligence—the kind of intelligence that provides a rich understanding about where your experience gaps are, because experience gaps are where neglect hides and where your untapped revenue opportunities lie. Naturally, you'll need better visibility into agent performance, customer satisfaction, and sentiment so that you can make better decisions about how to improve the experience you deliver to your NOW consumers. But you'll need (and want) more: intelligence that delivers real insights into how CX can become an engine of growth for your business.

NOW CX thrives on things like a closed-loop feedback, real-time reporting, and natural language processing that identifies clusters of like issues and analyzes sentiment. A NOW CX approach to business intelligence will take you beyond basic measures of efficiency and customer satisfaction to true business insights so that you can proactively enhance your customer experience and maximize every revenue opportunity. This is exactly what we will cover in *Part 4* as we explore next-level KPIs, how customer experience can attain its rightful place as a revenue center, and why CX should be driving your organization's business strategy.

NOW...

Let's get to work on blowing up the traditional contact center model and putting NOW CX to work for your organization.

PART 2

The Death of the Contact Center: The Birth of NOW CX

CHAPTER 4

Why the Contact Center Model Is Holding You Back

The Beer Game

Students at the MIT Sloan School of Management have been playing the beer game since the 1960s. While this might sound like just another Friday night on any university campus anywhere in the world, this particular beer game involves no actual beer.

Developed by Sloan's System Dynamics Group as part of Professor Jay Wright Forrester's research into industrial dynamics, the game simulates the beer industry's supply chain and illustrates the challenges inherent in the inefficiencies that plague any complex system. The beer itself is as incidental as it is imaginary. Professor Forrester's team might have built their simulated supply chain around widgets or wagon wheels but realized that theming and naming their game for many college students' favorite frosty beverage might pique a bit more interest. Over time, the game has become a rite of passage for first-year students at MIT Sloan, and has been played by thousands of other students, business executives, and government leaders around the world.

The premise is deceptively simple. A small team of four-to-eight players staffs four stations in a linear distribution chain, playing the roles of retailer, wholesaler, distributor, and factory. During each simulated business cycle ("weeks" that pass in rapid succession during one high-stakes night of gameplay), consumers "purchase" from the retailer, who then replenishes their supply from the wholesaler, who restocks from the distributor, who in turn orders and receives beer from the factory where it is brewed. All you need to do is meet customer demand by ordering enough from your own supplier, while avoiding costly backlogs and minimizing your excess inventory. When the players at all four points in the chain get the balance right, supply matches demand and the whole team's net profit soars.

When played competitively, the team with the highest profits— the result of a highly efficient supply chain that meets demand while minimizing waste—wins. And at MIT Sloan's annual beer game competition, the winning team walks away with both bragging rights and a pot of prize money. When Daniel* started his graduate work at Sloan, he couldn't wait to play (even if there wasn't any real beer involved).

There is one catch, though. Team members are instructed not to communicate with one another. Information is passed only through written orders and shipments that are passed only one link up or down the supply chain at a time. No matter how meticulous any one player is in keeping records of their own inventory, customer backlog, and open orders, they will still struggle with severely limited visibility into information across the entire system. Only the retail team members will understand true, real-time consumer

---

* Yes, the same Daniel who co-wrote this book. We figured that a temporary switch to a third person voice would be the least confusing way to signal that this story involves him directly and draws on his personal experience at MIT Sloan. Bear with us for a bit.

demand. Only the factory workers will know exactly how much beer is being bottled. The wholesalers and distributors in between will know neither, relying instead on their own inventory and orders to infer supply and demand.

Think of the beer game as a booze-themed version of *Telephone*. The miscues, miscommunication, improper orders, faulty calculations, and—significantly—the lag in timing between order and fulfillment as product moves up and down the chain worsen over time. Each stage in the team's supply chain falls further and further out of step with the others, resulting in confusion, chaos, and more than a few hypothetical broken bottles.

Still, when Daniel's own group of Sloan first years took their place among 50 or so competitive teams during their first shot at the beer game, they thought they would nail it. Just tell the person next to you *exactly* what you need and count on them to do the same. Right?

Wrong. Knowing what you know at this point you probably wouldn't be surprised to learn that Daniel and his teammates didn't fare so well. Even so, they consoled themselves that if they were to play again, knowing what they had learned about the rules of the game, they would walk away winners. That is, until they noticed how poorly the returning teams had done their second time around. The returning teams were awful too! Knowing the rules and having first-hand experience playing the game doesn't provide the advantage you might expect when the system is inherently flawed. And when those flaws stack the system against *you* and even your best efforts go unrewarded, it can be frustrating to say the least.

As Sloan Professor John D. Sterman once described, "During the game emotions run high. Many players report feelings of frustration and helplessness. Many blame their teammates for their problems... [Even] blaming the customer... is plausible. It is psychologically safe. And it is dead wrong."[1]

Your Losing Hand

If you're reading this book, you're more likely to work in customer experience than in supply chain management. But we'd wager that the challenges laid bare in the beer game still feel eerily familiar.

Like Daniel's team of MIT beer gamers, you once might have felt confident—even overly confident—that you and your company would step into the new world of high stakes CX and emerge victorious. You would work the system, crack the code, and deliver a level of service that would earn the business, trust, loyalty, and advocacy of an army of fans. In an age when customer experience is the primary battleground for business and the brand equity your company can build through phenomenal CX provides one of the few remaining competitive moats, a CX leader like you would be king or queen of the hill.

Why, then, does it feel like you're mired in the muck? Buried under a mountain of stress, frustration, aggravation, and dissatisfaction—your customers' *and your own*?

You might feel tempted to blame the competition for setting expectations unreasonably high, your colleagues for overpromising (*hello marketing!*) or underdelivering (*I see you, product development*), or your own NOW Customers for being so demanding. You may even blame yourself. *Don't!* To paraphrase a popular saying: it's not the players, it's the game.

You've been dealt a losing hand by the very nature of the traditional contact center model you've inherited. A service and staffing model built for the analog age—when telephone support was all the support anyone could ask for—has fallen woefully out of step with the demands of the digital economy. Sure, you can bend it, but it's already broken, and every choice you make and action you take will result in a costly compromise.

If you want to provide exceptional, responsive, always-on CX in an unpredictable market, the old contact center model requires you to constantly overinvest. It's the only way to keep bailing water from a leaky boat, even as management scrutinizes the ROI on every dollar spent. If you can't invest as much, you under-resource and attempt to deliver just enough to keep your brand one more interaction away from being torched by unhappy shoppers. Even if you could get that elusive balance right, the old CX model—one built around fixed headcount, hourly wages, scheduled shifts, operational inefficiencies, and high rates of attrition—makes attracting the best talent as difficult as attracting and keeping the best customers.

So, you've tried everything within your power to improve upon the CX model you've inherited: chatbots, self-help portals, offshoring, near-shoring, work-from-home policies, agent learning management systems, agent coaching software, different metrics and incentives, process redesign. You name it, you've done it. It feels like squeezing blood from a stone and, at the end of the day, none of it delivers quite what you need if you want to stand any chance of providing the experience you know your customers deserve.

To make matters worse, even the process of planning ahead is a predicament. Just like in the beer game, imperfect information about the state of your business and the disconnect between demand and supply hobble the contact center with two painful Achilles' heels. The number of people asking something of your company at any given time can vary by the moment, without warning, and often in a drastic way that catches you flat-footed.

So, recorded voices advise customers of *"longer than usual wait times"* as your company experiences *"unexpected call volume."* You respond to 95% of emails within four hours. But what about the other 5%, the one person out of every 20 who will need to wait longer than that? You manage to a 4.5-star experience, knowing that the fifth full star is out of reach. Even in the best of all possible scenarios, every trade-off is a trade down.

All of this begs the question: How do you get off this unpredictable treadmill and end this tiring tug-of-war so that you can deploy resources efficiently and still exceed the higher-than-high expectations of the NOW Customer?

The answer is as deceptively simple as the beer game's objective: *You choose a different model.*

Indeed, as we already suggested in *Part 1*, the companies that are winning the battle for consumers' hearts, minds, and wallets are already doing just that. They're breaking free from the traditional contact center model, the "every trade-off is a trade down" paradigm that too many other companies struggle with every day. And by treating the analog era support model like the relic that it is, they're making customer neglect a thing of the past.

In *Chapter 3*, we gave you a glimpse into the world of NOW era omni-channel customer experience, how it's different from yesterday's service model, and why it's the key to tomorrow's strategic advantage. And the rest of this book will guide you in making the shift to NOW CX. But before we dive into that, it's worth taking a closer look at how and why the traditional contact center model is keeping you from making the leaps necessary to meet your NOW Customers on their terms.

The Telephone Game

Although Alexander Graham Bell's voice first crackled over a telephone line in 1876, it wasn't until nearly a century later that most businesses got serious about staffing their own call centers. While individuals have certainly been promoting, explaining, and selling products and services over the phone since the start of the 20th century (maybe earlier), the call center as we understand it today didn't exist until 1965 when the UK-based *Birmingham Press and Mail* installed an automatic call distributor (ACD) system and hired a roomful of agents to solicit subscribers and field incoming inquiries.

In 1973, call centers hit the American mainstream when Continental Airlines installed a brand-new Rockwell Galaxy ACD and began booking tickets over the phone. As toll-free numbers were introduced in the 1980s, the pieces were in place for open communication between consumers and the companies with whom they did business.

Unbeknownst to customer service leaders of that era, it would be just a few more years before the deployment of a new technology called interactive voice response (IVR) would signal the beginning of the end for the traditional call center. While increasingly sophisticated IVR systems would make it easier for large enterprises to efficiently answer, screen, and route incoming calls at a scale that would otherwise require a not-so-small army of operators (a good thing, in theory), it would also make it possible for companies to deflect customer service inquiries with little more than the push of a button. And that's exactly what companies started to do.

We've already discussed the dangers inherent in deflection, the unfortunate and (frankly) odd strategy of actively avoiding the very people who are most essential to the success of the business, even to the point of neglect. Well, this is where it all began.

*   *   *

"Was there a time, pre-Internet, when it was acceptable to burn a single customer? To treat them so poorly that you'd sacrifice your next sale to that one person, without having much (if any) negative effect on your business overall," ponders Jeff Weiser, a former CMO with stints at both Shopify and Shutterstock who now serves as an operating partner at a consumer-focused private equity firm with investments in The Honest Company, Bliss, and Anthony's Coal Fired Pizza & Wings, among others. "Well," he continues, "If you look at the cold hard facts, it might be profitable just in terms of cost avoidance, or you might save a sale simply by making it harder to complete a return or cancel a subscription."

Naturally, Weiser doesn't *actually* believe this type of customer neglect was ever appropriate or productive (even if it could, technically, be profitable), but you can almost hear this kind of logic weighing in the minds of customer service executives as they institutionalized avoidance-by-automation.

As we'll get into in *Chapter 5*, we do believe there's a legitimate role for automation, but avoidance isn't it. *Press 1 for this. Press 2 for that. Press 0 to speak with a representative. Please hold (and hold and hold); your call is important.* Even in the late 1990s, as speech recognition systems started to replace old touch-tone technology and—in the interest of improving the experience—companies tried to provide a more pleasant, almost "human-like" interface for their customers, automation and self-service hindered connection more than it helped. We may have replaced key presses with voice prompts, but consumers quickly caught on: Automation was a trap. Even worse, it could be a time-suck as callers punched in or read out account numbers, zip codes, and the last four digits of their social security numbers, only to be routed (after the requisite wait) to a human agent who would request the same information again. Who among us relished the opportunity to call their cable company or insurance carrier? Or to ask about inventory, request a shipping update, or initiate a return?

But, to Jeff Weiser's point, maybe it didn't even matter all that much. Companies implemented these types of deflection strategies not for the customer's benefit, but for their own. Contact centers were one of the biggest cost centers for a typical company. Even a 1% increase in containment (the term applied to calls successfully deflected—or "contained"—in the IVR) could save a company millions of dollars over the course of just one year. The savings in salaries alone often meant that a company could realize a positive return on a typical automation investment in a matter of months.

It could be even worse when brands coupled cost-saving automation with low-cost outsourcing—putting customer relationships, trust, and loyalty in the hands of strangers (often halfway around the world) who would step their way through scripts but rarely summon the required levels of empathy, flexibility, creativity, or authority to resolve complex customer issues. Nicole France, former vice president and principal analyst at Constellation Research, recounts a personal experience that will hit home for anyone who has ever made an off-hours call to a company's toll-free number (and for any contact center manager who has ever sought relief through business process outsourcing):

> "When I lived in London, I had Internet service from Virgin Media. Overall, Virgin is known for creating great customer experiences, right? And I did indeed get great service whenever I called about an issue during regular weekday business hours because I would speak to a Virgin Media employee working in an in-house contact center right in the UK. They knew what was going on, they had access to engineers, technicians and the other parts of the business. So, they could really figure out what was at fault. Was it affecting just me or was my issue part of a bigger problem? Even if I couldn't get a quick resolution, I could get some good insight into what was actually going on.

> Any other time though, I would get routed to India. Don't get me wrong: The reps were lovely, very friendly, but they just didn't have access to the right information and couldn't get in touch with the right people. They were clearly trained to follow a script, so I rarely got to a resolution that was actually helpful and it was generally a waste of my time."

Probably not what Virgin intended. But much like in the beer game we described at the start of this chapter, imperfect information breeds ineffective action. And really, examples like this merely highlight the bigger issue. By the 2000s, deflection—to automated systems, to outsourced service providers, or to a combination of the two—was everywhere. For contact centers, this was the status quo—at a time when every other status quo was being challenged by major shifts in the way consumers connect, communicate, and do commerce.

As the world entered the 2010s—the first truly digital decade, the smartphone era, the age of the *FAANG* (Facebook, Amazon, Apple, Netflix, and Google) economy—automation and self-service went mainstream, everywhere from the airport to the minimart. Email, chat, messaging, and social networks came to rival the telephone as many consumers' primary point of contact with companies. These very same digital touch points and social media channels gave new voice to *Vocal Complainers* and *Social Media Megaphones*, as word of any single poor experience might spread to an audience of thousands. This certainly put new pressure on contact centers, raising the bar for efficiency, ease, and quality—and making every resolution a referendum on brand reputation. As Jeff Weiser puts it, "You're no longer dealing with the opinion, satisfaction or lifetime value of just one customer. You're dealing with fallout across all possible customers in all possible channels. You're not just satisfying one person or doing what you need to do to earn their next purchase. You're always thinking about what the spillover will be—positive or negative—so the burden to make everyone happy is that much higher."

Contact centers entered the age of digital customer experience but remained saddled with the same analog model and all of its constraints, without the resources, structure, or (sometimes even) know-how required to provide the rapid responses that electronic media requires. *Digital* deflection became the new norm. Emails could queue for days before an agent could respond. Chats were staffed during business hours only, leaving ecommerce primetime shoppers out in the cold. Tweets went unanswered. All of which only widened the gap between rising customer expectations and actual company experiences.

And this brings us back to the fact that, as a modern CX leader, you've been dealt a losing hand, saddled with an analog era service and staffing model that is unsuited to the demands of the NOW era digital economy and forced to make choices and take actions that require costly compromises you really can't afford.

The Only Thing Wrong with the Traditional Model Is Everything

We probably don't need to belabor all the ways the current contact center model holds you back or hammer home the kinds of compromises that are inherent in how contact center staffing works today. After all, you struggle with these things every single day. That said, we do think it's worth taking some time to cast a critical eye on what we see as the baked-in breakdowns in the traditional contact center. In a nutshell, six outdated attributes of the model result in a host of costly compromises.

Let's look at each of these challenges in a bit more detail.

Unscalable Contact Center Model	Costly Compromises
Fixed staffing	Backlogs, wait times, limited hours
Inaccurate forecasting	Unwanted deflection tactics, mismatch between capacity and demand
Outdated, ineffective approach to training	Long ramp time to proficiency, lowered productivity, risk of inaccuracy
Agents incentivized for efficiency over effectiveness	Agents incentivized for delighting the customer
Sky-high attrition	Wasted time/money training, knowledge loss, inconsistent customer experience
Rigid, scheduled labor model	Limited CX talent, low quality team

Fixed Staffing

Regular eight-hour shifts are not well-tuned to meet spiky, highly variable demand as it rises and falls over the course of any

24-hour period. While you might strike just the right balance
between staffing and volume at some point during the day, you will
invariably face two less than ideal scenarios at various points in any
shift. First, there will be times during which you have more agents
than you have tickets, with overstaffing resulting in waste. Second,
there will be times during which demand exceeds your capacity,
leading to backlogs, wait times, missed service level agreements
(SLAs), more deflection, and rampant neglect. The example illustrated by the following chart probably looks familiar to anyone
who has ever managed a contact center (or played the MIT beer
game, for that matter).

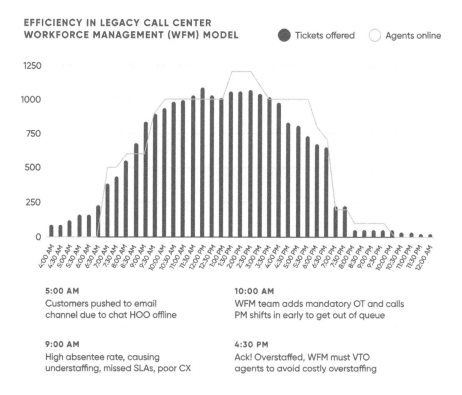

**EFFICIENCY IN LEGACY CALL CENTER
WORKFORCE MANAGEMENT (WFM) MODEL**   ● Tickets offered   ○ Agents online

5:00 AM
Customers pushed to email
channel due to chat HOO offline

9:00 AM
High absentee rate, causing
understaffing, missed SLAs, poor CX

10:00 AM
WFM team adds mandatory OT and calls
PM shifts in early to get out of queue

4:30 PM
Ack! Overstaffed, WFM must VTO
agents to avoid costly overstaffing

If this is a challenge even during most companies' so-called normal
business hours (9-to-5, Monday through Friday), the challenge is

compounded during nights and weekends. And again, the traditional fixed staffing model takes the blame.

As we've already noted, nighttime is prime time for many ecommerce businesses. Failing to adequately support *Late Night Browsers* would be roughly equivalent to a brick-and-mortar retailer leaving their stores unstaffed on weekends. So why is afterhours service a perennial problem for so many online brands? To answer this question, we spoke with Vincent Phamvan, chief marketing officer at careers platform Teal and a former Simplr teammate who spent more than a decade of his own career working in operations strategy roles and with contact center leaders:

> "Most people wouldn't question whether or not agents need to be available when customers are shopping. The hard part is that when you look at nighttime demand, you generally see something like a short, three-hour spike rather than a steady flow of tickets over a longer period. So, how do you match an eight-hour shift to a three-hour spike? You would have to staff some agents from 2pm until 11pm to catch incoming volume during, let's say, a typical 8pm to 11pm spike. You'd be ready for your nighttime volume but way overstaffed from 2:00 to 6:00. And, of course, you'd still be left without coverage between midnight and the morning."

When a contact center leader is forced to choose between being overstaffed during the business day or unavailable during busy evening hours, that's a textbook example of the kind of costly compromise CX teams make every day. Faced with stringent budget limitations (often set by someone in the finance department, far removed from the front lines of customer experience), evaluated on cost savings and efficiency, and struggling with the realization that she'd never get her best employees to work an inconvenient swing shift, the average contact center leader will opt for the status quo. And if it's hard enough to get the balance right on any given day, ow hard it is to accurately predict how many agents you'll need on a random Tuesday, two months in the future.

Inaccurate Forecasting

When your employer gave you your keycard, the odds are they didn't hand you a crystal ball. Yet, contact center leaders must spend an inordinate amount of time forecasting future volume—often 30, 60, or more days in advance—and attempt to achieve near-100% workforce efficiency. As director of digital operations, Jake Lechnir leads the guest feedback at Restaurant Brands International (RBI), one of the world's largest quick service restaurant companies and the owner of the Burger King, Popeyes, and Tim Hortons brands. When he sat down with us, he described a forecasting challenge that will sound familiar to any CX leader who has ever had to project future volume.

> "One of the biggest challenges is trying to predict what volumes are going to look like in advance. If you have historical data and your contact volume is consistent with that, the model can work. But for high-growth companies, volume can be very spiky. The traditional model breaks down if you have a large, sudden spike in contacts. You can't really predict these. And the traditional contact center can't staff up and down quickly enough, so you can end up with backlogs and an inconsistent experience for customers."

This kind of experience shows just how difficult it can be to get it right under any circumstance, but four factors conspire to make accurate forecasting a trickier proposition than it has ever been.

First, the kind of spikiness that results in under- and overstaffing at various points throughout any given day also manifests over the span of entire months and even seasons. Let's consider holiday shopping. Any consumer brand would reasonably expect increased volume during the last months of each year, but few can or will staff to meet *true* peak demand during this period. Vincent Phamvan explains, "Even if you know that Black Friday through Cyber Monday will be your true peak, that's just a few days. You can't staff to that level for just four days, and it doesn't make sense to staff to that level for the entire two months. So, you increase staffing over the holidays but only to your projected average demand across all of November and December. You go into it knowing that things are going to get hairy for four days but rather than properly plan for it you have everyone work overtime and try to do the best you can."

Even so, acknowledging the problem doesn't necessarily mean addressing it. Reflecting on a time before he had pushed his own organization beyond the traditional contact center model, Happiest Baby's Matt McCarron told us, "Back in 2018, we had a holiday season where we couldn't bottom out our queue for about three months. The only solution we had at the time was to hire, hire, hire. And we still had these incredibly painful months when customers were frustrated, and agents were burning out every day."

Second, contact center forecasts often fail to account for the unexpected events *at all*. Storms shut warehouses. Strikes slow down shipping. Websites and mobile apps fail. Product quality issues emerge. Pandemics disrupt every aspect of business as usual, which brings us to the next factor.

Third, few companies were prepared for the massive shift to online shopping that happened as the world went into COVID-19 lockdown and how this rapid digitization would raise the stakes for customer experience. And as we write this, many are unclear about the extent to which new post-pandemic digital behaviors will stick, whether ecommerce usage will remain at current levels, and the extent to which some sectors will see unprecedented surges in demand as parts of the world come in and out of pandemic-related restrictions and supply chain issues continue to plague a wide range of industries. In the face of this kind of ambiguity, nesses might opt to play it safe (even if over the long haul, they will be sorry). For some CX leaders, though, the signs are clear: COVID-19's impact on customer expectations are here to stay. Alexandra Vidaeff, head of client services at fashion brand FRAME, told us, "I think that people outside of CX think we can go back to the way things were before the pandemic, but that's not going to happen."

And fourth, automation factors into the forecast, as companies strive to offload a percentage of their volume to self-service solutions and/or chatbots. But there is actually more guesswork involved here than most would like to admit. As we'll see in *Chapter 5*, chatbot buyers may be overly optimistic about the volume of tickets that can be resolved by technology without human intervention. On top of that, self-service is only as good as your customers' willingness to use it, which in turn is a function of how well you've implemented it. And then, when making ends meet to fit the available budget, it's too easy to make pat assumptions about the extent to which customers will shift from live agents to on-demand FAQs, voice assistants, or other automated options (e.g., *"Let's take last year's self-service rate and bump it up by 5% to hit the budget on paper, even if we don't know if this will happen in practice."*)

The bottom line is that forecasting can be as much art as it is science, inaccuracy is almost inevitable, and the fixed staffing model means that too many contact centers are forced to understaff rather than overspend—always at the expense of the customer experience.

Outdated, Ineffective Approach to Training

In the traditional contact center model, agents are trained in two main ways. Both are flawed. First, a new recruit undertakes a rigorous upfront training curriculum designed to convey essential skills and accelerate their ramp to proficiency—the amount of time it takes for a new agent to match the performance of the average agent in the call center. This said, it's simply not possible to teach somebody everything they need to know in order to do their new job well, so from the start companies must make a calculated trade-off between selective know-how and comprehensive knowledge. To make matters worse, not every new agent who begins training will make it through to the end of the program. In other words, you're paying to train a lot of people who never even take their first customer call. This kind of drop-off is an early warning sign of a larger agent retention issue.

For those that do complete training and take their seat at a contact center desk, additional training hours may be delivered intermittently (typically, a few hours each month) but with the recognition that every minute spent learning is a minute not serving a customer. Because of this trade-off, ongoing training hours are as likely to be cancelled as they are to be kept—especially if the contact center is understaffed, metrics aren't being met, or the CX budget gets cut. Phamvan likens this to skipping your annual physical. "What happens if you cancel it once? Probably nothing. How about twice? You're probably still going to be fine. But if you cancel it 10 times in a row, that's when you might really start having issues that your doctor could have spotted sooner. The same logic holds true here. You cancel training a few times and figure it's not a big deal. But over time, on-the-job performance really suffers." And with it— we'd add—so does the customer's experience with your company.

Agents Incentivized for Efficiency Over Effectiveness

Another troublesome holdover from the cost center way of thinking is that customer service agents aren't paid particularly well. So, one historically popular way to combat low compensation has been through bonus incentives that are, in theory, attainable by any agent—*provided that they work fast enough to get their customer off the phone or chat.*

To show what we mean, let's walk through an example of

something we've seen all too often among large contact centers. Most customer service leaders have learned that they can't simply offer bonuses based on the number of calls or chat inquiries their agents take, as there's a plethora of ways to game that system. So, they instead determine bonuses based on a combination of efficiency metrics (like call, email and chat volumes) and quality metrics (like a CSAT survey sent to customers following a service inquiry). To keep things interesting, they'll often layer in a level of competition, pegging bonuses to each agent's relative performance relative to their peers. In other words, the top 10% of agents earn their full bonus, while those in the lower brackets get less.

If you think this sounds like a smart way to ensure both quality and efficiency, think again. Savvy (or maybe sketchy) agents will quickly learn that speed is still the surest way to ensure consistently high bonus pay, because efficiency can be controlled to a much higher degree than quality or effectiveness. Agents will accelerate escalation on inquiries that they know will be long in duration. They will find ways to avoid incoming inquiries on products that typically have long chat times, while rushing to take inquiries that they know can be resolved quickly and with high customer satisfaction (like forgotten passwords). They will deflect to an FAQ or piece of content as a first step. And by doing so, they will guarantee that they will perform exceptionally well for the chunk of their bonus that is determined by efficiency. Any positive CSAT scores that come in are just icing on top.

Meanwhile, agents that focus on quality or aim to achieve a balance between quality and efficiency are in far less control of their own financial destiny. First, quality interactions can inherently take more time and require more effort. Displaying empathy, personalizing the conversation, or offering additional support outside the initial scope of the call are almost mutually exclusive to the concept of pure speed. By attempting to gain a few points on quality, they lose points on efficiency. Second, for agents who focus on quality to influence their compensation, there is no guarantee that their efforts and time will be worth the work. You could offer exceptional service and still receive a low CSAT simply because the customer was in a bad mood. The bottom line is that, in general, agents that are speedy tend to be compensated better than those who are more customer-minded—even when their bonus structure attempts to control against that outcome.

CX leaders who wish to drive real revenue from support and service interactions must go beyond this outdated way of thinking about incentives and focus instead on rewarding the agents who drive resolutions in a way that both delights the customer and maintains the quality of the brand. This means first and foremost making resolutions the key metric, and then layering in a level of quality assurance and accuracy to enforce good behaviors among agents. As Hannah Steiman, chief operating officer at Peak Support, has written, "If you only incentivize quantity or speed, quality will suffer as agents focus on volume to the detriment of everything else. Even incentivizing speed and customer satisfaction isn't good enough. An agent could get a great CSAT score by giving refunds to anyone who asks—but that doesn't necessarily mean she's doing her job. A good incentive pay system should incorporate productivity targets; customer satisfaction; and a Quality Assurance score that reflects other performance metrics important to the company. If you don't have a fully developed QA program, you might want to build one before adding incentive pay."

In *Chapter 9,* we'll take another look at why auditing customer inquiries and measuring quality (not just completion) are so important.

Sky-High Attrition

Traditional contact centers struggle to retain employees. This challenge is so extreme that, according to Phamvan, many customer service departments turn over close to 100% of staff during a typical 12-month period. It's worth considering why this is the case.

ContactBabel, an analyst firm for the contact center industry, attributes attrition to a wide range of factors: poor hiring, lack of opportunities for advancement, boredom with repetitive work, excessive pressure and stress, dealing with unpleasant customers every day, high numbers of temporary staff (often hired during predictable peaks only), poor working conditions, low pay, and the general availability of other legacy contact center roles.[2]

When we discussed these challenges with Phamvan, he echoed ContactBabel's rundown of the issues plaguing contact center staffing, noting that the last two factors can be particularly insidious. "A surprising amount of turnover actually comes from somebody leaving one call center to go to another call center," he said, "It's not a matter of getting a better job. It's just a matter of earning a few cents more per hour to do essentially the same job." In a sense, the vast majority of traditional contact centers offer undifferentiated and unappealing work environments that struggle to attract, then fail to retain, the best possible representatives for your brand. When faced with the possibility of small incremental bump in pay, contact center workers are more than willing to trade like for like.

This dynamic forces CX leaders to spend an inordinate amount of time, energy, and resources on recruiting, hiring, and ramping new employees who may soon take whatever knowledge they've gained with them as they head for the exits. Worse, this dynamic often contributes to glaring inconsistencies in the experience you offer your customers.

The consequences of high attrition are undeniable. And we believe attrition (not to mention recruitment) is about to get worse.

Rigid, Scheduled Labor Model

The on-demand economy hasn't merely raised the bar for customer experience. It is also actively reshaping the workforce in ways that make it harder than ever before for contact centers to attract and retain top talent.

For years, people have been buzzing about the gig economy—"a global market where companies and contractors (independent workers) set short-term and on-demand professional relationships that are both flexible and skill-based."[3] More and more workers— even the most qualified workers among us—opt for the flexibility of independent, non-traditional work arrangements over the more stable yet often wearying grind of the 9-to-5 work week. We are going to explore this trend in detail in *Chapter 6.*

**INCREASE IN CALL CENTER ATTRITION
AND ON-DEMAND ECONOMY WORKERS**

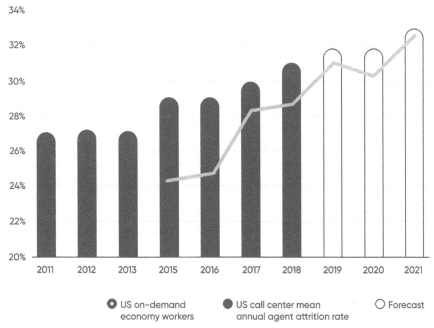

Sources: 4, 5, 6

For our purposes here though, it's important to note that any contact center staffing model that relies exclusively on regularly scheduled shifts that are worked in a structured, onsite office environment will only become increasingly out-of-step with the flexible conditions that top talent demands. In fact, we are already seeing contact center attrition rise alongside the steady growth of the on-demand economy, gig work, and online talent marketplaces such as Lyft, Mechanical Turk, Upwork, TaskRabbit, and Fiverr. Similarly, it isn't hard to imagine that we will see an increase in the difficulty of traditional contact centers attracting qualified talent.

Having said all this, even this macrotrend doesn't account for another way in which rigid, scheduled contact center staffing may already be preventing you from attracting certain high potential pools of qualified talent: military spouses, retired or semi-retired white-collar workers, former executive assistants, well-educated stay-at-home parents or family caregivers, and school teachers looking to supplement their income on nights, weekends, and holidays—or people with disabilities or other conditions that might preclude them from working in a traditional contact center environment.

Now, here's where this gets interesting: The growing disconnect between the contact center's rigid labor model and the increasingly flexible workstyle sought by workers may be a pain point for you today. But tapping into (rather than bucking against or—just as bad—ignoring) the trend toward flexible, on-demand work will be one important way that the NOW CX model reimagines the delivery of customer experience for tomorrow. In *Chapters 6* and *7*, we'll be taking a deeper look at the rise of the flexible workforce and how you can use it to your advantage.

But first, given all the ways in which people problems stand in the way of customer experience excellence, it's probably worth asking...

Can You Win the Contact Center Staffing Challenge?

The bottom line is this: You *can't* win the contact center staffing challenge any more than Daniel could win the MIT beer game. At least, not without blowing up the traditional contact center model. And that's exactly what we're here to do.

The good news then is that the legacy model for delivering customer service doesn't need to be *your* legacy. NOW CX can and should be. And given that (as we've seen in this chapter) staffing challenges underscore so many of your day-to-day service struggles, it's fitting that the journey toward NOW CX begins with reimagining talent. Flexible, scalable, and always-on. Empowered by technology not as a means of deflecting volume or containing customers, but as a way of enhancing the speed and quality of human-first engagement.

We hope you'd agree that this detour into the past and consideration of the present was worthwhile, just to be sure we're on the same page about where we are today, how we got here, and why we need to break the mold. The rest of this book is about creating the future of customer experience, at your company and as an industry.

CHAPTER 5

Wait, I Thought Bots Were the Answer

Who's Calling, Please?

Google CEO Sundar Pichai paused midway through his keynote at the company's I/O 2018 conference as a telephone conversation between two women played out over the sound system in Mountain View's Shoreline Amphitheatre. The exchange itself couldn't have been more mundane: An executive assistant is heard booking a haircut for her busy boss as the salon receptionist on the other end of the line offers up different options in an attempt to find an appointment that accommodates the executive's availabilities. But the audience sits in rapt silence throughout, before exploding into enthusiastic applause as Pichai lets them know that the salon worker had been speaking with Google Assistant, not a human admin, the entire time. Google Assistant, running a conversational artificial intelligence called Duplex, spoke, listened, and responded so naturally—even reacting appropriately to unexpected new information without missing a beat—that the human receptionist never knew she was speaking to a machine.

Although Pichai made it clear that Duplex was, at the time, very much still under development and actually quite limited in terms of the different interactions for which it had been trained, this demonstration illustrated the potential for truly conversational AI. It signaled that the kinds of thinking machines that had been a longtime mainstay of science fiction—from *2001: A Space Odyssey*'s diabolical HAL to Theodore's chatbot love interest, Samantha, in Spike Jonze's 2013 film *Her*—might finally be capable of conducting routine conversations between a company and its customers. And in the years since 2018, we've seen no shortage of chatbot providers who are quick to pitch customer service teams on the promise of slick, seamless conversational technology that would allow their organizations to automate interactions with buyers.

In practice, though, today's most prevalent chatbot solutions are closer to Eliza than Duplex, Samantha, or even (frankly) Amazon's Alexa.

Wait, Who's Eliza?

In 1966, the German American computer scientist Joseph Weizenbaum introduced the world to Eliza, one of the earliest examples of a computer program that could simulate conversation with human users. In other words, Eliza was a chatbot. Arguably the *very first* chatbot.

Running a script called "Doctor," programmed to mimic the open-ended back-and-forth between a psychotherapist and patient, Eliza would engage human users in text-based conversations by applying pattern matching rules to simulate personalized, relevant, one-on-one dialogue. Although Eliza was quite a rudimentary bot, people who interacted with her were often wowed by her intelligence and level of understanding. Some attributed humanlike emotions to her, even if they already realized she was a computer program.

But Eliza's intelligence and certainly her emotions were mere illusions that could be easily dispelled by steering the conversation into areas that Weizenbaum hadn't programmed into the Doctor script. Unlike today's AI, Eliza could not learn from interactions, gain new skills through experience, or pick up on new patterns of speech through conversation alone. She could process and parrot the content of a sentence but not truly understand the context or even the meaning of the individual words. For example, if a human user were to type in the well-known proverb, "Necessity is the mother of invention," Eliza might reply, "Interesting. Tell me about your mother."

This type of communication breakdown was less surprising to Weizenbaum than the extent to which people could be duped into believing that Eliza was a sentient machine. Not only did he know the limitations of the technology that he had developed; he had actually developed it not to test the degree to which human-machine interactions could be meaningful but to "demonstrate that the communication between man and machine was superficial."[1]

Granted, bots and AI have come a long way since 1966. But even today GPT-3 (Generative Pre-Trained Transformer 3), a massively powerful AI that generates text that is indistinguishable from copy written by a human and is widely considered to be one of the world's most advanced examples of machine intelligence, is "largely a mirage," according to MIT Technology Review writer Karen Hao. She explains, "You can tell with a simple trick: Ask it the color of a sheep, and it will suggest 'black' as often as 'white'—reflecting the prevalence of the phrase 'black sheep' in our vernacular"[2] but ignorant of the fact that an actual black wooled sheep is quite rare in nature. Needless to say, few of us are running artificial intelligence as powerful as GPT-3 anywhere in our businesses today (it's quite experimental and still considered to be in beta as we write this), and AI like this certainly isn't powering the chatbots at work in our contact centers. For that matter, many chatbots don't use AI at all (more on this in a bit).

So, let's be honest. More than 50 years after Joseph Weizenbaum published the Eliza chatbot, you can still detect a bit of her DNA even in Amazon Alexa, every time your Echo Dot blares "It's Raining Men" by The Weather Girls after you ask it to read out your local weather report. And your ecommerce customers recognize that they're getting something less than Google Duplex when the bot on your website answers their questions about a given garment's fit by linking to a sizing chart but can't quite empathize with their complaints about COVID-19-lockdown weight gain.

We don't mean to dismiss outright the role of chatbots in delivering modern CX. After all, technology is a core pillar of the NOW CX model and bots (along with other tools for automating parts of the experience) can be a powerful means of moving beyond conventional approaches to support, delivering better service through consumer-preferred digital channels, and increasing buyers' access to your brand. But we do think that it's important to ask whether customer service chatbots are a means to being more meaningful or just one of the many ways CX leaders compromise by settling for being superficial.

Ultimately, the answer lies in how you use them and what kinds of conversations you're trying to handle. But first, let's consider why the idea of automation sounds like a path to the promised land of NOW CX—and why the reality so often falls short of the mark.

The Benefits of Bots

At face value, chatbots appear to address three key challenges that many companies face in meeting the demands of the NOW Customer.

The Need for Speed

Often a customer only needs to know they've been heard. They have a simple question and need a simple, fast response. In addition, more times than not, the majority of inbound emails, texts, and chat messages are about the same subject. You may not need a customer support agent to handle these and repeat the same answer over and over again. In situations like these, chatbots are able to provide rapid replies with little to no lag between the inquiry and the answer.

In fact, speed is an ideal use case for one common type of bot: the autoresponder. Autoresponders work over email and chat to serve up near real-time responses based on text analysis of incoming questions or requests, never taking off time for nights, weekends, or holidays. Which leads us to the second potential benefit of bots.

Always-On Availability

Chatbots allow organizations to provide 24/7/365 service without ramping up staffing or adding around-the-clock shifts. Essentially, bots help eliminate the disconnect between your daytime business hours and your customers' prime nighttime shopping hours while mitigating the effects of unexpected spikes that leave human customer service teams struggling with backlogs.

Consider the ways in which self-service chatbots let a buyer use text-based web chat to find answers for their own questions without speaking directly to a human representative—especially in situations or at times when a human representative may not be readily available (nights, weekends, holidays, during surges in demand). Simple self-service bots may be little more than transactional—providing single touch responses and directing customers to pre-loaded FAQs, helpful articles, or relevant product pages—but can certainly be effective in that context. More sophisticated examples strive to be more conversational, using multistep decision trees to sustain back-and-forth dialogues as they guide consumers toward the information they need and—ultimately—toward a resolution.

Some of your customers may actually prefer to serve themselves in this way. As Shannon Jimenez, senior customer support manager at virtual presentations platform mmhmm explains, "Millennials and younger consumers in particular will go to your website and try to find answers on their own." But more broadly we know that customers (regardless of generation) absolutely prefer always-on access that makes it easier for them to get the answers they need, when and where they need them, without having to even consider availability or wait times.

Overcoming Resource Inefficiencies

By diverting ticket volume away from human agents, chatbots may decrease the need for brands to hire additional staff and can reduce the CX leader's struggle to plan for unexpected peaks and valleys in demand. On paper at least, bots represent a lower cost means of growing an organization's CX scale, flexibility, and capacity—all while taking on rote requests and freeing human agents to focus on more complex tickets. Within the context of a hybrid customer service scenario that empowers humans with technology, bots can also be helpful for collecting information about an inquiry upfront and (when set up correctly) routing that information to an agent, thereby saving time, reducing repetitive fact-finding, improving response speed, and resulting in better issue resolution.

* * *

Salesforce global innovation evangelist Brian Solis highlighted these same advantages of automation when he wrote, "Chatbots can field repetitive tasks, like routing cases to the right agent and answering simple questions. Done right, they free employees to focus on more creative, valuable work, while giving customers fast responses even when case volumes are high." Factors like speed, availability, efficiency, and scale are certainly compelling benefits of automation in general, and chatbots in particular—especially if they can be achieved at a fraction of the cost of hiring, training, and retaining agents. This is great.

But...

The Big Bot Buts

Companies that implement chatbots for customer experience—especially companies that have unrealistic expectations about how well bots will solve for key CX challenges—often find that the reality falls short of the promise.

For starters, chatbots excel at efficiency but generally fail at empathy. You'll remember from *Chapter 1* that NOW Customers demand more than speed. They also crave a certain amount of human connection, even if conversation is secondary to more transactional needs such as access to information during the purchase process or rapid resolution of post-purchase complaints.

But when it comes to infusing automated interactions with even the most basic elements of human understanding, bots miss the mark—resulting in an unsatisfactory and frustrating customer experience. In *How to Scale Your Chatbot*, Forrester Research analysts Vasupradha Srinivasan and Leslie Joseph explain:

"Consumers want convenience, not conversation. But chatbots still fail to fully deliver even when they source information effectively. Users are often guided to a page or link for more information. Even when bots are configured to understand user queries, parse documents, and respond with specifics, it's common to copy information from the source and paste it into a chat with no real attempt to infuse it with AI or make it conversational. The user ends up with a complex statement from a written document and a link for additional information — which, ironically, comes off as more robotic than conversational. This reduces customer satisfaction effectively and dissuades them from ever coming back to the chatbot, rendering the channel ineffective. For chatbots to be scalable and effective, conversational AI must actually be conversational."[3]

The simple truth is that most chatbot solutions lack the ability to deliver personal, empathetic interactions with buyers. The more complicated truth is that many chatbot solutions are built around rules, not artificial intelligence—and that this imposes a strict limit on the extent to which a bot can be truly helpful in a customer's moment of need.

Rule-based bots—by far the most widely deployed type of chatbot today—hold basic conversations based on if/then logic, without actually understanding context or intent. Like Joseph Weizenbaum's Eliza, these bots are scripted by human trainers: agents who map typical conversations, set up flows, and program decision paths based on common questions and their associated answers. From here, the chatbot will only work within the scenarios for which it was trained—it won't learn through interactions, get smarter over time, or offer answers outside of those predefined in the rules. All of this makes it difficult (and in some cases, impossible) for rules-based chatbots to handle inquiries that are highly specific, have multiple parts, or are more complex, ambiguous, or unique to a given customer's situation.

Now, this isn't necessarily *bad*, but it does relegate the role of the bot to information delivery more than issue resolution. And it does mean that, in practice, customer service organizations often find that their chatbots have significantly lower take and resolution rates—not to mention, higher escalation rates—than they had anticipated.

In fact, some industry analysts have estimated that less than 10% of customers can fully resolve their issues or accomplish their desired task via automation or self-service. Here at Simplr, our own conversations with CX leaders at well-known ecommerce brands bear this out.

One manufacturer of outdoor products loved the idea of automating a significant portion of their customer interactions, but the experience ultimately left a lot to be desired for both the company and its consumers. While they expected their chatbot to resolve roughly 30% of all in-scope tickets, it could only handle 10-15% of volume. To make matters worse, the brand quickly noticed that when the bot *was* involved in conversations, CSAT scores suffered—an obvious CX red flag. Similarly, when a rapidly growing male grooming brand saw initial success after assigning 11% of their ticket volume to a chatbot, they attempted to increase that share to 35%—only to learn the hard way that their bot couldn't actually resolve much more than its original 11% allocation.

So, we have a situation in which chatbots promise speed and always-on availability, but in practice take on less volume than you might expect, resolve fewer issues than you'd hope, and hurt the quality of your customer experience more than you can afford. Now, let's consider automation's promise of better resource efficiency, and why the reality may actually be quite different.

We've already hinted at the amount of time, resources, and effort that go into setting up rules-based bots. More broadly, current self-service systems rely heavily on humans to create and maintain them—mapping flows, writing responses, reviewing and updating the underlying knowledge bases, and so on. Other forms of automation—for example, Robotic Process Automation (RPA)—are equally dependent upon humans to identify, understand, document, and convert workflows that can be performed by software. Ironically, all of this is still quicker and easier than training an AI-based bot—an effort that today requires a massive amount of data and can take years before the bot can reliably and responsibly handle a wide range of scenarios. Ultimately, Forrester cautions that even rules-based "chatbots may need months of care and feeding before they're capable enough to handle a meaningful proportion of inbound queries"[4]—a time-consuming and costly proposition that cuts against the notion that automation will free your customer service team to focus on higher value buyer engagement and eats away at the savings you might realize by automating support.

At the same time, chatbots' low resolution rates and the very fact that they set the expectation for always-on customer service combine to create a scenario that could actually *increase*, rather than decrease, your need for human agents. Many, if not most, chatbots (including those that incorporate some form of artificial intelligence) are designed to escalate to a human agent when technology alone is unable to resolve an issue, when they cannot confidently identify or understand the customer's intent, or when they encounter a situation with which they are unfamiliar. In a perfect world, this takes place in a seamless *human-in-the-loop* handoff and results in an engaging, productive, and even profitable customer interaction.

At a time when bots can reliably and responsibly handle just 10% of customer conversations (give or take), it's incumbent on brands to maintain adequate staff to pick up the remaining 90%, either at first contact or via a chatbot hand-off. And (here's where it gets tricky) at a time when your bot is on the job 24/7/365, you'll need agents available to take those hand-offs all day, every day—including on nights, weekends, and holidays—regardless of your traditional contact center's business hours. "It's ultimately about providing a consistent experience for customers across all channels," explains RBI's Jake Lechnir. "A company can't move toward more self-service without considering how their customers can simply and seamlessly connect with a real person any time—and I'll stress *any time*—they need a response or a resolution beyond what technology alone can offer."

Companies that fail to operate this way fail their customers, opening the door to even more opportunities for customer neglect. Clearly, this is nobody's intention when they enter the world of chatbot automation, but it is an unexpected consequence of mistaking chatbots for *the* answer to NOW Customer expectations, rather than considering chatbots as just one component of a robust NOW CX strategy. Naturally, we have a perspective on how to get the role of chatbots right.

A Resolution on Responsible Automation

Don't get us wrong: We're not saying that there isn't a time and place for chatbots and other automation solutions. There certainly is. After all, Gartner has found that 70% of consumers use self-service options *at some point* in their resolution journey.[5] Supporting key digital channels like chat and email through automation is one means to better meet the NOW Customer on their terms and at their time.

The problems generally arise when an organization over-indexes on automation at the expense of issue resolution. It's easy to be lured in by the promise of speed and around-the-clock support, then blinded by the cost savings. So much so that you might lose sight of the long-term implications for the quality of your customer experience, the level of customer effort, the effects on customer loyalty, and the impact on revenue. When the way you employ bots amounts to little more than one more way to deflect volume away from your customer service representatives, automation becomes just one more cause of customer neglect.

Clearly, customer-facing automation needs to be used responsibly. The question is, "How?" Forrester distills the formula down to this: "Let customers choose their preferred channel, limit chatbots to simple questions, and carefully craft the escalation path to a human."[6]

In practice, this means relying on automation alone only when you feel 100% confident that the technology can provide a satisfactory resolution and reduce the amount of effort required on the part of the customer. And it means that wherever and whenever chatbots or other forms of automation are at work, you're also providing your customers with access to—and a quick, seamless handoff to—human agents if and when they need it. If your company offers 24/7/365 chatbot support, your customers expect 24/7/365 *human* support. It really is that simple. And for any conversation that is complex, complicated, high-value, high stakes, or consultative in nature, you'd be wise to opt for human-first engagement. Otherwise, the cost savings of automation likely aren't worth the potential lost revenue or the high cost of customer neglect.

When you consider that just 10% of typical company's consumer inquiry volume can be handled by a bot today, the hybrid staffing model might look something like this:

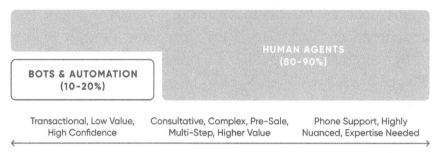

BOTS & AUTOMATION
(10-20%)

HUMAN AGENTS
(80-90%)

Transactional, Low Value,   Consultative, Complex, Pre-Sale,   Phone Support, Highly
High Confidence   Multi-Step, Higher Value   Nuanced, Expertise Needed

FULL SPAN OF TICKETS

Now, we'd be the first to tell you that the ideal balance between humans and technology is not static over time. With automation and artificial intelligence continuing to improve, chatbots will become increasingly capable of handling more and more complex conversations, reading customer intent and understanding context, and even approximating empathy and mirroring human emotions. The boundaries between human support and automated service may blur as truly intelligent "digital humans" (AI beyond bots) take on an overwhelming majority of even your thorniest customer contacts.

Still, for CX leaders today, if bots *aren't* the answer (yet), what is? The short answer is technology *plus humanity*. Or more precisely, humanity augmented and empowered by the right technologies. And this brings us directly to the rise of the flexible workforce, the power of the "human cloud" and the future of service beyond the contact center.

CHAPTER 6

The Rise of the Flexible Workforce Changes Everything

Employee Experience Is (Almost) Everything

J. Willard Marriott, founder of the global hospitality company that bears his name, once said, "If you take care of your people, your people will take care of your customers and your business will take care of itself." The Container Store's co-founder Kip Tindell raised the stakes when he said, "Take care of employees better than anyone else and they will take care of customers better than anyone else." And in his signature style, Sir Richard Branson once declared, "Clients do not come first." If this last quote sounds like heresy to anyone committed to customer experience, rest assured he was just putting his own spin on the idea that employees come first: "If you take care of your employees, they will take care of the clients."

In fact, the direct link between employee experience and customer experience (and for that matter the link between employee experience and company performance) has been obvious for some time. In its 2017 Employee Engagement Benchmark Study, Qualtrics XM Institute drew a direct connection between high employee engagement and above average CX, finding that "seventy-nine percent of employees who work at companies with significantly above average customer experience in their industry are highly or moderately engaged, compared with only 49% at companies with average or below average customer experience."[1] In that same year, future of work strategist Jacob Morgan found that companies that invest in employee experience are four times more profitable than those that don't.[2]

These are just two data points among a growing body of evidence that supports the tie between employee experience (EX) and CX. As Enrique Rubio, founder and CEO of Hacking HR, notes in an article on SAP's The Future of Customer Engagement and Experience website, "To be able to give that ultimate world-class experience to your customers, you need to build it inside your organization. We can't give what we don't have, right? But data shows that when your employees are engaged, treated with dignity and respect, valued, and offered opportunities for growth within your organization, they embody those values and pass them onto your customers."[3]

The article goes on to note that "the opposite is also true. Workers who feel unappreciated, mistreated, or ignored convey their dissatisfaction to customers. And unhappy employees who don't put your customers first won't help your company meet its goals or drive desired business outcomes."[4]

It's hardly surprising that the well-known customer experience futurist Blake Morgan (incidentally, Jacob Morgan's better half) calls the connection between EX and CX "*un-ignorable*."[5] And yet, it seems that most contact center managers still ignore it.

All of this begs the question: *How good is the employee experience in your CX department?* If the sky high (and rising) attrition rates driven by poor hiring, lack of opportunity, boredom, excessive pressure and stress, and low pay are any indicator, the honest answer is, "Not very." And as we pointed out in *Chapter 4*, it's not likely to improve if customer experience remains tethered to the legacy contact center model. Instead, CX leaders have an opportunity (even an obligation) to rethink what it means to work in customer experience and redefine the CX employee experience to be more in line with modern workers' expectations for work.

As we'll explain in *Chapter 7*, the leap to NOW CX begins with capitalizing upon the rise of the flexible workforce, arguably the most significant talent trend shaping the future (and present) of work. With that in mind, it's worth considering just how much work is changing overall before exploring how you can turn this trend into your employee experience advantage.

Rethinking Work

In the years since journalist and editor Tina Brown coined the term "gig economy" in a 2009 *The Daily Beast* article, the knowledge workforce that earns its living through "a bunch of free-floating projects, consultancies, and part-time bits and pieces while they [transact] in a digital marketplace" [6] has evolved into a sector that by some estimates is worth as much as $1.2 trillion dollars today.[7] Size aside, the emergence and growth of the gig economy—sometimes called the freelance economy or on-demand economy, and closely associated with the sharing economy named for the access-over-ownership business models of platforms like Uber, Lyft, and Airbnb—represent a radical rethinking of the nature of employment, the definition of career, and the shape of the global workforce.

Matthew Mottola and Matthew Coatney are two of the leading thinkers charting the shift toward the on-demand workforce. In their book, *The Human Cloud*, they liken this new, uniquely digital way of working to the shift technology infrastructure has undergone, from owned and on premise to remote, shared, and in the cloud: "The *human cloud* is the platform by which people and businesses can easily and quickly find and work with other people in a digital, remote, and outcome-based way. Consider it the 'office in the cloud' since it translates everything that happens in a physical office through a digital equivalent."[8]

Through this lens, the gig economy becomes more than a clever label for temp work, side hustles, and stray projects. It serves as the seed for a more meaningful movement that has the potential to make an on-demand, highly skilled talent pool as accessible and scalable as distributed computer processing power and data storage are today.

Enter the Expert Economy

Even if we look beyond the world of Uber drivers, Instacart shoppers, and DoorDash delivery people, it might be tempting to dismiss the gig economy as the domain of low skilled, low commitment, even low-quality workers. Acceptable for stray projects but unsuitable for strategic work in the core of the company. Even Tina Brown cast a skeptical, satirical, somewhat dismissive eye upon the burgeoning gig workforce in her seminal column.

It's important to nip this misconception in the bud. *This* is not *that*. We sat down with *The Human Cloud* co-author Matthew Coatney to learn more about how he sees the virtualization and variability of work playing out today.

"We're seeing this market movement of freelance talent, where it's not just a matter of offshored, low value work. It's high value professionals. It's accountants. It's lawyers," Coatney explained. Consider, for example, how the legal talent platform Axiom matches highly credentialed, on-demand attorneys or even entire tailor-made outsourced legal teams with corporate law departments that need capacity, expertise, agility, or scale beyond what their in-house staff offers. Coatney went on to tell us, "We're talking about people in any industry who are at the top of their game, who have made a choice to work with multiple clients at once and not be tied to an individual employer. We think of this as the expert economy. That's a more accurate term than gig or even freelance."

And just as the two Matthews do in their book, Matthew Coatney suggested that every leader should be asking themselves and their peers inside their organization, *"What could we do if we had a world of experts in our pocket?"*

This begs two questions:

1. First, is on-demand expert talent really that abundant (*a world?*), given that highly skilled workers seem to represent a relatively small portion of the freelance economy today?
2. And second, should we be thinking of great customer service representatives as experts?

* * *

To the first point, the Matthews argue, "As the office increasingly digitizes and embraces remote work, we'll all work like freelancers. This means we'll all control where we work, when we work, and what we work on."[9] Even if you might be skeptical that their use of the word *all* smacks of hyperbole, estimates peg contingent labor at somewhere between 40% and half of all white collar workers today, while a pre-pandemic study commissioned by Upwork and the Freelancers Union projected that the size of the on-demand workforce will surpass that of the full-time workforce by 2027.[10] This should come as no surprise when you consider that contingent expert workers already outnumber full-time employees at some of the world's most forward-thinking organizations, like Google.[11]

So, the expert economy (and more broadly the rise of the flexible workforce) is happening, and it's going to be big. We think it's worth exploring the factors shaping this trend because they are the very same factors driving your need to reject the rigid and fixed contact center model and reimagine your customer service team as a scalable and always-on flexible workforce.

Digital and Technological

The emergence and evolution of digital talent marketplaces like Upwork, Catalant, InnoCentive, and Toptal have made it easier than ever for independent experts to find opportunities and organizations to source experts. At the same time, cloud-based applications make it possible for workers (employed, independent, or otherwise) to be productive on their own and collaborative together, regardless of employment status or location. As Mottola and Coatney write in *The Human Cloud*, "Software is shifting our relationship with work from being physically present in real-world local networks (think within an hour of your home and office) to being digitally present in a virtual, global, limitless network (the internet and relevant applications)." All of this blurs the boundaries of the organization, making the distinction between full-time and freelance less meaningful.

But the impact of the digitization of work goes well beyond practicality and productivity in two important ways. First, it makes the unbundling of high-quality talent from the permanent workforce more important today, in part because of the extent to which automation is taking on the routine, rote, and repeatable functions that comprise such a substantial portion of the typical employee's daily duties. When we spoke with Matthew Coatney, he told us, "All of the easy problems are being solved with technology. So, all that's left for humans are the thorniest, most complex, most sophisticated asks. When you look at this within the context of customer experience, you can imagine how this creates a clear need for more experienced, higher quality CX talent at a time when many contact centers and BPOs are squeezing their internal teams for cost savings and optimizing for machine-like efficiency."

Second, it forces workers and employers to reevaluate the relationship between humans and machines, and to recognize that the future workforce will be truly hybrid. In their book, the Matthews write that a "*machine cloud* is the yin to the human cloud's yang. Instead of accomplishing tasks with only humans, the machine cloud can perform or support many tasks through automation and artificial intelligence... Straightforward tasks (and increasingly complex ones too) are handled by machines, freeing [humans] up for the really meaty work. It's not about saving the time of the task itself but also the mental switching cost of going from simple task to simple task."

While on the one hand this echoes what Matthew Coatney told us about the effects of automation, on the other hand it speaks to the promise of *augmentation*. When you equip skilled workers with the right technologies, you enhance their ability to perform tasks efficiently, effectively, and with excellence. And when you free human workers from the drudgery of low-level work that can be handled by machines—freeing them to focus their intellect and energy on the so-called *meaty* stuff—you clear the path toward a workstyle that is more meaningful and a workforce that is more engaged. This leads us to the second set of factors shaping the flexible work revolution.

Social and Personal

According to one recent article in *Harvard Business Review*, "Millennials, who are already the largest generational cohort in the workforce, tend to be tech-savvy and to prefer to work for themselves rather than for traditional organizations. They want more autonomy and control over their job security than previous generations had."[12]

At the other end of the generational spectrum, an aging population means that more seniors are choosing to work later into life, and experienced retirees are exploring unconventional opportunities to supplement their income on their own terms. Savvy companies like UPS and Target are already tapping into this trend by building their own "flexforces" of on-demand ex-employees and retirees who can "boomerang back on a contingent basis to fill important skill gaps."[13] Amazon has been doing something similar for over a decade through its CamperForce program that attracts migrant RVers—many in their 60s and 70s—to fill thousands of seasonal warehouse positions during peak periods of demand (the Oscar-winning film *Nomadland* cast CamperForce in the spotlight, as Francis MacDormand's character, Fern, packed Prime orders in Amazon's Nevada facility before hopping in her van and driving into her next stint of life on the road).

And in between Millennials on the rise and Boomers on the road, we have everyone else. According to one study by Intuit and Emergent Research, "Many people have a desire and both a financial and psychological need to have multiple sources of income. In an era when pensions, unemployment benefits and other social services are changing, many Americans view on-demand work as a way to create their own financial stability."[14] For some, the decision to work on-demand is a necessity, for others a choice. And for others still— single parents, sandwich generation caregivers, military dependents, women spending time outside the workforce, and more—flexible work can provide fulfilling opportunities when rigid, place-based, 9-to-5 roles are not a realistic option.

And Then There Was COVID-19

Everything we've been looking at so far predates the start of the pandemic that forced organizations around the world to adopt remote work policies that proved (at least to some extent) that local physical presence may not matter so much in a world where commerce is increasingly global, digital, and virtual. And now, as the pandemic recedes and companies contemplate partial or total returns to the office, upwards of 40% of workers are thinking about quitting their jobs[15]—a potentially massive amount of churn that economists have dubbed "the great resignation."

While any individual employee might have their own motivation for moving on after a year or more of learning an entirely new way to work, it is undeniable that the desire for greater flexibility and autonomy will factor into a significant number of decisions. As University of Michigan economist Betsey Stevenson told Axios, "People have had a little more space to ask themselves, 'Is this really what I want to be doing?' So some are deciding they want to work fewer hours or with more flexibility to create more time for family or hobbies."[16] Add other post-pandemic patterns—like the urban exodus, the host of small towns around the United States that are offering relocation bonuses to remote workers who no longer need to live within commuting distance of a corporate headquarters, and the rise of digital nomads—and it becomes clear that COVID-19 has accelerated the shift that was already underway. The shift, that is, toward a substantial pool of experienced skilled labor that favors work that is more flexible, fluid, varied, independent, rewarding, meaningful, and tech-enabled than most full-time employers can offer.

The Expert Economy Fosters Extreme Ownership

Now, you might be thinking that this is all well and good, but wouldn't a flexforce worker be less responsible, less committed, and less engaged than a full-time employee who earns a regular paycheck from your company? According to Mattola and Coatney, no.

In *The Human Cloud* they write, "The human and machine clouds create a fundamentally different relationship between work and us. We're no longer beholden to office politics. And we can no longer hide behind the job title and short list of responsibilities. Today, we're naked, with our track record visible for the world to see... The human cloud thinks playing hide-and-seek with your merit is unfair. Which is why it puts every single one of us on one network that's global, transparent and quantified."

This transparency in turn creates a culture of *extreme ownership* among skilled professionals who have chosen a career of on-demand expertise. Now, these contingent workers obviously don't own your business, your brand, or even the customer relationship. But they do own the outcomes they create. And to the extent that those outcomes reflect on their reputation, credibility, and desirability on the open market, high quality delivery of the services they provide become their stock in trade.

Consider how this might contrast with the typical contact center employee, ground down by the system and going through the motions. And consider that the level of pride on-demand experts take in their own achievements (and the ways in which this could translate into better interactions with your company and its customers) is just one advantage the flexible expert workforce provides to organizations that embrace it.

Your On-Demand Opportunity

It's no secret that employers are engaged in a war for talent. Even as pandemic-driven unemployment soared, millions of roles remained unfilled as companies struggled with skill shortages. And in this era of rapid automation and rampant business transformation, even new skills have a shrinking shelf life, and a widening digital skills gap threatens to become a strategic bottleneck for many organizations.

As a CX leader, you've likely struggled with this yourself to some extent. Consider how challenging it can be to find and hire the best customer service talent, how difficult it can be to cross-train seasoned telephone agents to context switch between multiple digital and social media touchpoints, and how frustrating it is to stem attrition and prevent your best workers from job hopping to another contact center around the corner. And now, think about how hard it is to find the right people with the right skills at the right time to meet a short-term spike in customer demand—assuming you even see that spike coming.

In scenarios like these, access to an on-demand skilled workforce becomes a strategic advantage. And leaning into a new way of working benefits more than just the employee. It offers your organization a greater degree of flexibility, agility, scalability, and access to a more diverse pool of skilled talent that might otherwise not be available on a full-time basis.

Writing in *ComputerWorld*, Paul Gillin notes that an on-demand workforce gives employers "unprecedented flexibility in marshaling human resources," as long as companies "think of contingent workers as extensions of their full-time workforce rather than disposable piece parts. This attitude change will only become more important as gig labor becomes more entrenched—a trend that has accelerated in the last year from business' growing comfort level in hiring remote workers... In a world dominated by contract labor, success depends less on hiring the best people than on *having access to* the best people."[16]

On the one hand, the rise of the flexible workforce exacerbates the war for talent, as more and more educated and experienced experts choose to work outside traditional corporate constraints. On the other hand, the rise of the flexible workforce provides savvy, forward-thinking organizations with a powerful new weapon with which they can win that war. Leaders responsible for staffing business functions as diverse as the technology team, the legal department, finance, innovation, and marketing are already finding a strategic advantage in on-demand experts.

Now, how about you? That depends on how you answer the second question we posed earlier in this chapter.

Should We Be Thinking of Great Customer Service Reps As Experts?

The answer, of course, is yes. In fact, that's exactly what we call our flexforce workers here at Simplr. But more generally, the best customer service reps are expert communicators, expert listeners, expert problem solvers, and expert relationship builders. They're experts in identifying opportunities to cross-sell and upsell and experts in turning a bad experience into a successful resolution—a pathway to loyalty and basis for advocacy. And naturally, they're experts in how to use the tools and technologies at their disposal to achieve all these things quickly, efficiently, effectively, and with empathy.

In fact, if there's anything customer service reps *don't* need to be experts in, it's clocking in and out of your traditional contact center. And this is where your ability to access an on-demand workforce as part of your overall human capital strategy creates an opportunity to break free of the contact center model.

Now that you understand the broader trend toward flexible work, let's turn our attention to exactly how moving to a more flexible, scalable, and always-on approach to CX staffing empowers you to eradicate neglect and better meet the needs of the NOW customer.

CHAPTER 7

Moving From Rigid and Fixed to Scalable and Always-On

Partly Cloudy

As you learned more about how businesses tap into the flexible workforce, you might have been thinking: "Wait, aren't we already doing this?" And the truth is that, to some extent, maybe you are. But there's a wide gap between the two most common ways the CX industry has been leveraging gig customer service and the *new* way we'd recommend that you tap into the expert human cloud. And we're certain that the ways most organizations are approaching gig labor today not only fall short of the true potential of the flexible workforce, but they also reinforce (rather than overcome) some of the drawbacks baked into the contact center model. Let's take a closer look at the CX sector's two historical gig work approaches:

- A form of business process outsourcing (BPO) that relies heavily on gig workers to handle customer service inquiries, a model known to be problematic both for workers and for the brands they serve.

- Crowdsourcing "superfans" who use their personal experiences with a brand to respond to customer service inquiries, a model with natural limitations.

And let's explore why these approaches offer neither the truly flexible, engaging work environment that today's expert flex workers demand, nor the quality and scalability your company needs in order to rise to the NOW CX challenge.

The BPO Gig Customer Service Model

The BPO customer service model relies largely on outsourced customer service representatives to provide companies with better coverage—both in terms of active hours (up to 24/7/365) and additional channels—and potentially shorter response times.

Ironically though, the outsourced construct of these BPOs does not allow for the flexibility that companies and gig workers seek. Outsourced contact centers rely on scheduling labor, much like internal contact centers do. This is a flaw that prohibits scalability and requires long-term contracts that make it challenging for companies to quickly and cost-effectively scale up or down based on fluctuations in customer demand. In essence, this construct replicates the confines of an internal contact center model.

The Traditional Crowdsourced Superfan Model

Superfans are a hard-earned gift to any brand. These passionate outside voices use their social media channels to amplify and advocate for their favorite products and services. Some gig customer service platforms let brands take this fandom to a new level, leveraging superfans as an extension of customer service teams who can reply to consumer inquiries based on their own relationship with the company and experience with its products or services.

While true fans can certainly convey brand appreciation and be the voice of product experience, there are some distinct limitations. The reliance on tribal power user knowledge is limited by personal preferences and opinions that can become static, leaving some super-fans unprepared to adapt when brands rapidly evolve their products and brand messaging (as many have done in response to shifts in consumer needs, preferences, or expectations, especially in the wake of the COVID-19 pandemic.)

By its nature, this model pulls from a shallow labor pool, leaving the burden of recruiting talent on the brands themselves. This can work for a company that has a substantial fanbase or a robust partner community that builds and maintains a network of fans willing to take on this type of gig work. But for any company that doesn't already have that community with deep product and service knowledge, this approach is a non-starter. And even if a company does have a substantial pool of superfans, without a sophisticated unified communications platform it remains a challenge to scale that support, providing 24/7/365 digital coverage that is equal parts knowledgeable and responsive. Inherent limitations like these make it hard for this gig approach to have the scale required to take enough customer service volume to be meaningful, preventing it from mainstream adoption. Additionally, without a large following of fans that only a select few companies can boast, the model can't be utilized by companies of all types and sizes.

Despite the inherent and obvious limitations of these two approaches to gig CX, the use of contingent workers in staffing customer service departments is becoming more and more acceptable among online retailers, direct-to-consumer brands, and (particularly after the pandemic increased the need for instant-on scalability) practically any company regardless of industry or business model. But for customer experience teams to truly make the leap from yesterday's rigid contact center model to tomorrow's flexible NOW

CX strategy, they'll need to do more than choose a business process outsourcer or put their brand into the hands of fans. They'll need to tap into the human cloud.

A Sunny Outlook for the CX Human Cloud

In *Chapter 6* we touched on the advantages that the human cloud offers for both experts and employers. Here, we'd like to take a more detailed look at the benefits of this flexible, scalable, always-on model for customer experience departments specifically. While there are a range of benefits—including the relative ease of recruiting, the speed to hire and ramp new talent, and more—we'd like to focus on two advantages likely to have the greatest impact on your bottom line.

Human Cloud Agents Are Happier Agents

It's no accident that we started our exploration of the human cloud by noting the direct link between employee experience and customer experience. Customer care agents who work in an on-demand workforce are more likely to be satisfied with their jobs and more engaged in their work.

Traditional domestic call centers have always been plagued by the high attrition and absenteeism associated with poor working conditions and low wages. As we've already noted, these factors also contribute to low morale among BPO support agents and often impact the quality of the support they provide to your customers. In fact, lack of flexibility is one of the main reasons cited for absenteeism in legacy call centers. Unsurprisingly, significant levels of staff absence can cause major problems with contact center performance, and ultimately the customer experience.

Additionally, the disruption caused by natural disasters, weather events, or the COVID-19 crisis can be devastating for workers (and the brands they support) who are unable to travel to work or whose call center has suddenly closed. This is especially apparent today for companies who rely on offshore support teams. The absences caused by these catastrophes—through no fault of the labor force itself—can wreak havoc on worker morale and cost organizations a significant amount of time and money to rectify.

On the other hand, people who choose to work in the human cloud have far more control over their work-life balance than those who are required to report for their shift at a contact center. When independent contractors in the customer service industry "come online," they bring their most optimal selves to the job. There are also fewer restrictions on career or personal development. Support team members can pursue other career opportunities or start a family while still logging in anytime they'd like. As more workers seek opportunities that better align with their priorities, purpose, motivation, and lifestyle, this type of flexibility is hardly trivial; it is a powerful draw for in-demand, on-demand talent that might otherwise be outside the reach of the typical contact center manager.

In her Constellation Research analysis of the human cloud workforce that powers Simplr's NOW CX solutions, Nicole France noted, "The typical expert is a well-educated U.S. citizen (a good many have advanced degrees) who demonstrates strong problem-solving abilities. These are people who value flexible work schedules and can resolve or escalate customer queries quickly... From my perusal of Glassdoor, satisfaction levels seem to be high among Simplr experts. Unsurprisingly, the ability to define work schedules and duration for themselves ranks high among the job benefits."[1]

Naturally, we believe we've done a good job of building a top-quality network of on-demand CX experts. And as Nicole noted, our Glassdoor ratings bear this out.

Company	Glassdoor Rating
Simplr	4.8
Concentrix	3.9
Arise	3.8
Working Solutions	3.8
LiveOps	3.6
TTEC	3.5
Sutherland	3.5
Sitel	3.4
Teleperformance	3.5
Sykes	3.3
Alorica	3.0
Convergys	3.0

Source: BPO Glassdoor ratings as of January 2021, using Glassdoor's proprietary algorithm and each company's overall rating based on the quantity, quality and consistency of reviews during the period of eligibility.

We also know that the ability to attract and engage higher caliber workers is a fundamental benefit of the human cloud in general. Shannon Jimenez, senior customer support manager at video presentation platform mmhmm, saw this firsthand when her prior company was a Simplr partner. When we spoke with her about her experience with Simplr's human cloud network, she told us, "There are real professionals who have spent years working in support, but due to a life change can't do a nine-to-five. But they can work a couple of hours at a time, here and there. We wanted to help these people, give them work. At the same time, our brand benefitted from having access to their on-demand expertise when we needed to scale support."

Let's move on to the second benefit of the human cloud for customer service.

The Human Cloud Provides Perfect Efficiency

In *Chapter 5*, we discussed the disconnect between spiky demand and fixed staffing as a fundamental (and we'd argue, fatal) flaw of the legacy contact center. We noted that a traditional staffing model that is shift-based and heavily dependent on full-time employees results in periods during which the contact center is over- or under-resourced. When CX is managed for efficiency (a bigger challenge that we'll take on later in this book), the imperfect dynamics of fixed staffing put CX leaders at an inherent disadvantage.

We shared the following chart, and you might remember the sense of unease you felt as you noticed the periods during which staffing dipped below demand or available capacity rose above actual ticket volume.

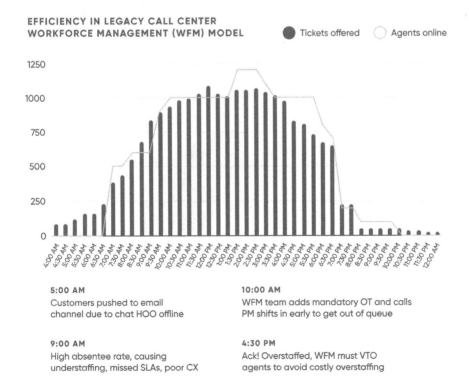

EFFICIENCY IN LEGACY CALL CENTER
WORKFORCE MANAGEMENT (WFM) MODEL   ● Tickets offered   ○ Agents online

5:00 AM
Customers pushed to email
channel due to chat HOO offline

9:00 AM
High absentee rate, causing
understaffing, missed SLAs, poor CX

10:00 AM
WFM team adds mandatory OT and calls
PM shifts in early to get out of queue

4:30 PM
Ack! Overstaffed, WFM must VTO
agents to avoid costly overstaffing

Now, let's contrast this with a flexible, on-demand, and instantly scalable CX staffing model, powered by the human cloud. No staffing model can improve the accuracy of your forecasting, but the human cloud goes a long way toward making forecasts obsolete. Your company growth or seasonal trends create a surge of tickets and you need to scale? Great, turn up the dial! (Or rather, let the dial turn itself.) Need to cut back on your customer support team? No worries. In the on-demand model, work is distributed among a large team that works across multiple client brands, and no one will get offended (or evicted, for that matter) if scaling customer service for you means temporarily scaling downward. These same dynamics, unique to the flexible workforce model, apply whether a given surge or dip in demand lasts for one month or one minute. As a result, when properly implemented as a key component of your CX workforce strategy, human cloud staffing matches available agents to ticket volume and delivers perfect efficiency, as illustrated below.

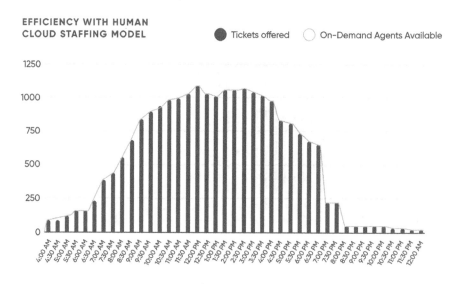

So far, so good. But what happens when you couple variable staffing with variable compensation? It gets even better.

While salaried contact center workers are compensated for hours spent on the job each week (even if their performance might ultimately be evaluated based on their ability to efficiently field and resolve customer inquiries), flexforce experts can be engaged and paid based on proven productivity. By paying independent agents on a per-resolution basis, you're only staffing and paying for the work needed at your company.

*   *   *

By now, it should be clear that intelligent, on-demand CX staffing is convenient, effective, efficient, and more attractive than ever before given the burgeoning movement toward a human cloud-powered expert economy. But can integrating the human cloud into your CX staffing strategy actually work in practice? Can customer experience truly be improved by an army of independent agents? And is this the case even if your customer support issues are complex or you already have a good team of in-house agents?

To answer these questions, we'd like to share an example of one company that's already tapping into the human cloud as part of their NOW CX approach—and discuss how the approach they've taken can be applied by any customer service organization as a practical framework for making the leap from rigid, fixed, and staffed in shifts to flexible, scalable, and always-on.

Happiest Baby's Formula for Happy Customers

At first blush, Happiest Baby sells SNOO, the premium $1,500 smart baby bed and a range of accessories to round out parents' purchases. But ask Matt McCarron and he'll tell you that their real benefit to customers is *peace of mind*. As he told us, "When a new parent connects with one of our agents, they're not merely calling about our products. They're calling about the most important person in their life. Sure, if their baby isn't sleeping then they want to know if our product is right for them, that their purchase is working the way it's supposed to or that they're using it correctly. But more than that they need to hear that they're on the right track and that they're doing a good job as parents."

As you might imagine, these high stakes and emotionally fraught conversations might call for a special kind of customer service representative. One who can provide clear, accurate information and resolve issues efficiently, but who can also exhibit true empathy (and often sympathy) in every interaction. "The last thing you want to do is churn and burn through your calls with these parents," says Matt.

In contrast to the traditional contact center model, Happiest Baby employs a team of sleep consultants who have both the expertise needed to solve real infant sleep challenges and permission to do the job right. "The average call with one of our sleep consultants lasts about 30 minutes," Matt explains. "As you know, in the traditional customer service model, the *last* thing you want is a 30-minute call. You want to keep your transactions down to two or three minutes, right? But if we're going to coach a parent on specific tips and tricks for their baby, we really need to take our time, listen to them, figure out what will work for their infant and for them as parents, and—again—make sure they feel understood."

Listening to Matt describe his company's approach to deep-dive customer care, we can't help but recall Zappos' groundbreaking policy that allows for unlimited call times. As an employee explained in a blog post on the footwear and apparel retailer's own website, "Customer service calls at Zappos take as long as they need to take. Length of calls are not limited or dictated by company call time parameters. If a customer needs help with product fit, we can work with them to figure it out. If a customer needs assistance with their shipment carrier, we can contact [the carrier, with the customer] on the line. And if a customer needs to exchange everything in a 19-item order—there's plenty of time to do that, too."[2] It's a policy that has made Zappos legendary for customer experience. And it's a policy that was put to the test in 2017 when two different customer loyalty team members each clocked individual calls that lasted nearly 11 hours (yes, *hours*!).[3]

But as Matt realized early in his tenure overseeing customer care at Happiest Baby, half-hour expert-led consultations (as important as they are for the mission-driven baby brand) are neither required for *all* calls nor desired by *all* customers. For every customer looking to have a detailed conversation, you might have a dozen looking for quick answers. So, Matt asked himself, "How can I design a system where a certain type of ticket doesn't result in a massive backlog for other ticket types?" He found the right answer in a NOW CX strategy that combines an in-house team of experts with the unprecedented flexibility of the human cloud and the instant-on benefits of properly deployed self-service technology. In a nutshell, Happiest Baby's CX staffing strategy has three main components:

- Automated self-service through an always-on chatbot that answers frequently asked questions and offers commonly requested information by guiding shoppers to specific articles and assets in a robust library of online content.
- A dedicated team of in-house subject matter experts who focus on the most complex cases and most nuanced issues, typically over the phone during a pre-arranged consultation.
- A distributed, on-demand network of freelance CX agents who provide around-the-clock support for customers across key digital channels like Instagram and email while serving as the first point of escalation from the automated chatbot channel.

Matt describes this approach as being *multi-lane*, designed to efficiently route each customer to the service model that meets their immediate need. He is also quick to describe it as "where a lot of companies are going in the future." We agree. In fact, we believe that a multi-lane approach to customer service staffing—one that relies heavily on your ability to tap into an on-demand workforce while still making smart, strategic use of automation—provides companies with an opportunity to break free of the legacy contact center model that no longer serves them or their customers. So, let's draw on Happiest Baby's experience to look at how a flexible and scalable multi-lane staffing model can work for you.

Multi-Lane: The Onramp to NOW CX

Near the end of *Chapter 5*, we introduced what we consider to be a realistic, workable split between human agents and technological automation. We based it on the current state of chatbot intelligence (at the time of this writing, that is) and some of our clients' real-world experience with bots. As you'll recall, the division of labor across a full span of typical ticket types looked like this:

	HUMAN AGENTS (80-90%)
BOTS & AUTOMATION (10-20%)	

| Transactional, Low Value, High Confidence | Consultative, Complex, Pre-Sale, Multi-Step, Higher Value | Phone Support, Highly Nuanced, Expertise Needed |

FULL SPAN OF TICKETS

Think of this as a *two-lane* model with traffic split roughly 80/20 (at best) between agents and automation. Rather than reiterate the advantages and limitations of chatbots, we'd like to take a few moments to note the elegance of Happiest Baby's approach to automated support as it provides a smart model for delineating a clear, viable role for technology in a human-first NOW CX model.

When a visitor engages Happiest Baby's chat channel, there is no illusion that they're speaking with a human. While the bot bears a human name (Melissa), it's quick to inform customers that they're dealing with a machine, then provide a clear idea of the types of simple queries it's best equipped to handle by offering a succinct list of common topics. While a shopper might choose to interact with the bot through free text, the quickest path to a successful resolution comes by pointing and clicking through a series of either/or options (e.g., a shopper curious about discounts will be asked to choose between two discount programs: one for healthcare professionals, one for military), each designed to guide the shopper to a specific webpage or on-site article that provides the most relevant information. Any time a customer's need becomes too complex for Melissa or within seconds of a "speak to a human" request, Melissa offers several escalation paths (live chat, email, or telephone call-back) to put the customer in contact with a real person.

This brings us to the human agent part of the equation—the real people tasked with handling the vast majority of all interactions. Today, for most customer experience organizations—organizations employing a two-lane model and beholden to the legacy contact center model—these real people come in the form of high turnover employees (sometimes complemented by a contracted BPO's employees and gig workers), scheduled in shifts and managed to minimize cost. This is the CX status quo that is riddled with inefficiencies and plagued with a range of costly compromises—an inability to scale up or down to match spiky ticket volume, poor coverage or slow response times across digital channels and outside regular business hours, inevitable backlogs, and rampant customer neglect.

And this is where moving from two lanes to three, making the flexible workforce a core component of your CX staffing strategy, delegating tickets between two different but equally qualified set of experts, comes into play. With a multi-lane hybrid model, the CX staffing framework would now look something like this:

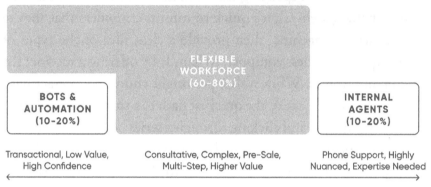

BOTS &
AUTOMATION
(10-20%)

FLEXIBLE
WORKFORCE
(60-80%)

INTERNAL
AGENTS
(10-20%)

Transactional, Low Value,   Consultative, Complex, Pre-Sale,   Phone Support, Highly
High Confidence   Multi-Step, Higher Value   Nuanced, Expertise Needed

FULL SPAN OF TICKETS

In this multifaceted approach to full coverage, the role of automation doesn't change—with bots handling the transactional, low value interactions that can be most easily automated—but the role of your own internal agents might, as they rise to the challenge of solving customers' most sophisticated challenges. In the Happiest Baby example, we saw a clear use for internal agents: lengthy, nuanced infant sleep consultations that require a unique blend of expertise and empathy, problem solving ability and patience.

As you think about how to deploy your own internal agents, you might ask: What is the nature of your company's most nuanced, sophisticated, or complex customer conversations? Which interactions require the highest level of expertise, what transactions carry the highest stakes, and which relationships warrant extra attention? What CX opportunities and challenges are best handled over the phone, where true real-time, one-on-one dialogue provides the greatest likelihood of a successful resolution?

While these are just a handful of the questions you should consider when designing a workforce strategy that allocates ticket volume between in-house and external agents, one thing is certain: The answer is never "all of them." And so, in our multi-lane framework, the flexible workforce provides enough external CX experts to handle the wide range of tickets that exceed the abilities of automation but don't quite call for the unique, highly nuanced expertise offered only in-house. And it does so with perfect efficiency, appropriate empathy, around-the-clock availability, and instant-on scalability. While many of the tickets routed to the flexible workforce might pertain to common issues, questions, or requests, populating your flexible network with customer experience experts rather than lower-level gig workers means that this external extension to your team can also be prepped and primed to handle higher value, more consultative, multi-step interactions with success.

For Matt McCarron, a flexible workforce provides him with "peace of mind" that mirrors the peace of mind Happiest Baby offers stressed-out, sleep deprived parents. RBI's Jake Lechnir frames the same benefits as "spike insurance," highlighting the comfort he gets in knowing that no inquiry goes unanswered, and no customer gets deflected or deferred, even when actual tickets exceed his forecasted volume.

Naturally, determining the split between in-house and flexible agents depends on the specifics of your business. In the three-lane framework we've presented above, we've pegged the split at somewhere between 10-20% internal and 60-80% external (with the remaining 10-20% falling to automation). But the truth is that the ratio will vary widely, depending on the nature of your business and complexity of your customers' needs.

When he was at Shopify, Jeff Weiser (you met him back in *Chapter 1*) says, "A large percentage of our full-time headcount were customer care 'gurus' because a big part of our innovation was that we made this complicated thing—running a profitable online store—easy and intuitive for merchants that might otherwise be intimidated by technology. So, it was important that we had a large team of people with deep subject matter expertise in everything from the most specific features of our platform to big picture advice on how to attract buyers." At the other extreme, the head of ecommerce at a $200 million athleticwear brand confided that her company employs only one in-house customer service expert; all other inquiries can be handled effectively by a flexforce of external reps.

Regardless of where your own organization falls on this spectrum (most likely somewhere in between, and we'd wager closer to the split in our framework), breaking free of the problematic hire-then-fire, churn-and-burn, trade-offs-and-trade-downs legacy contact center model requires building or buying into a flexible workforce.

The Human Cloud, CX Style

We'll be blunt. You cannot make the leap to NOW CX unless you commit to embracing on-demand experts. The question is, then, "What does an effective on-demand organization look like for customer service?" Here at Simplr, we've built our entire business model around helping companies in a variety of industries move CX to the (human) cloud, so we naturally have some strong perspectives about how any organization can get it right.

- The human cloud is digital-by-definition, making cloud workers uniquely suited to handle most (or even all) of your digital touchpoints: email, chat, messaging, and even social customer service. They can pick up where your bots leave off, while freeing your internal staff to prioritize the most complex, involved, or unanticipated queries that often benefit from more phone time.
- Opt for experts over low-level gig workers. As we've described, the changing world of work has led more and more experienced professionals to pursue contingent work relationships. For example, while at Constellation, Nicole France wrote, "A typical [Simplr] expert is a well-educated U.S. citizen (a

good many have advanced degrees) who demonstrates strong problem-solving abilities. These are people who value flexible work schedules and can resolve or escalate customer queries quickly."[4]

- Strike the right balance between onshore and globally distributed. U.S.-based businesses recognize the benefits of having access to onshore, native English-speaking experts, but also understand the value of a widely distributed global network that is ready to work outside regular U.S. office hours. After all, one of your main goals is to provide 24/7/365 service. For example, our network employs many military dependents stationed at locations across North America and on bases around the world, giving our U.S.-based clients the best of both worlds: local agents and follow-the-sun global coverage.

- Embrace performance-based compensation. And as we noted earlier in this chapter, adopting a pay-per-ticket resolution (the kind of outcome-based compensation common among gig workers) not only supports the scalability of the model and the cost effectiveness of your investment in a human cloud. It moves your entire CX operation toward waste-free efficiency.

- Empower your flexible workforce with technology. In the same way that the machine cloud and human cloud go hand-in-hand to power the expert economy overall, a sophisticated technology platform is key to the human cloud customer service model.

In a sense, this last point is a corollary to our point that the human cloud is digital-by-definition. And it's worth a few moments to go a bit deeper into why it's vital that your on-demand workforce operates as a truly networked team, empowered, and augmented by a robust digital platform. This platform is, of course, different from the use of chatbots, self-service and other automation tools to intercept customer contacts and deflect volume away from human agents. Here, technology is the means for improving human-to-human interactions.

App-based, AI-powered knowledge bases and online collaboration software are just a few solutions that make it easier for contingent workers to learn the business and succeed in it. The right platform also integrates with your core systems, permitting seamless context switching. It allows on-demand experts to take on digital customer service tickets with machine learning-enabled guidance that's provided in the moment. In other words, even without the type of lengthy and often ineffective training required for internal agents, an outside expert can log into the platform and take a ticket for your brand (or any other brand, for that matter) and immediately respond based on the guidance that appears on their screen, whether it's a question on a return policy, product availability, order status... You name it. They'll have the answers they need, served up in a brand-appropriate look, voice, and tone.

A technology platform like this makes it easy for both companies and on-demand workers to take full advantage of the flexibility inherent in the human cloud. Companies can ramp up the number of inquiries they share through this technology platform as they see fit and on-demand workers can log on when and wherever they want, responding to as many customer inquiries as they can handle.

The Heart of the Conversation

In *Chapter 5*, we asserted that the answer to your contact center staffing woes was not technology per se, but the combination of technology and humanity. And this is exactly what you put in place when you combine all three parts of this multi-lane approach: sensible automation for the most rote and routine inquiries, in-house human agents for the most involved conversations, and a digitally enabled on-demand CX workforce for every customer contact in between.

And when you get this right, you achieve a lot more than just smarter staffing. You take your first bold step away from the legacy contact center model that holds you back from delivering truly modern CX. And you begin the process of transforming routine customer questions and complaints into real opportunities for conversational commerce. In the next section, we're going to explain exactly what we mean and how this important shift puts your CX organization on the path to becoming a vital driver of revenue *and strategy* for your entire organization.

PART 3

How the Best CX Teams Become Revenue Centers and Strategy Drivers

CHAPTER 8

How NOW CX Transforms CX from Cost Center to Revenue Driver

Are We the Champions?

"How do we champion the support team and show people across the company it's not a cost center?" asked Phil. Shannon started to reply but paused, thinking maybe she had misheard the question.

Sensing her hesitation, Phil clarified, "In other words, what can we do to show the organization that there's so much value in having a good support team, and in providing our customers with a great experience, that your function is seen an essential driver of growth?"

For context, we should point out that *Phil* is Phil Libin, the cofounder and CEO of video communications company mmhmm. *Shannon* is Shannon Jimenez. And this exchange (ok, we've dramatized it a bit because who doesn't love a good story?) took place during her first meeting with her new boss, after joining mmhmm as the startup's senior customer support manager. Phil's question was a new one for Shannon, and seeing it as an opportunity to elevate the perception of customer service at her new company, Shannon took it on as one of her first challenges.

When we spoke with Shannon, she told us, "In my prior role, I had a world class team, but so much of the focus was on volume and efficiency that we never had the chance to think about demonstrating a higher form of value to the organization. And to be honest, in that kind of environment, it can be hard to think of a metric that you can show the company. On a sales team, you can see revenue. You can see that the customer success team is reducing churn. With customer service, even if you survey customers or show overall satisfaction through CSAT or Net Promoter Score, it can be incredibly difficult to draw a direct line to revenue."

And to be fair, before Phil, no other senior executive had ever challenged Shannon to reimagine her customer service operation as a revenue center. In fact, very few organizations are having this conversation at all. Nicole France—whose work at Constellation Research gave her visibility across a wide range of CX teams in virtually every industry—confirmed to us, "The people in charge of service and support haven't widely enough socialized how essential it is that customer experience is not viewed as a necessary evil that should be as cheap as possible. Leaders across the entire organization need to see it as a crucial means of driving relationships, revenue, growth and profitability."

While it's certainly advantageous for your customer service function to be *viewed* as a means of driving those things, it's even more important to *actually drive them*. The former requires a robust set of KPIs by which you measure your contribution to the business and a savvy approach to communicating your success up and across the company. The latter requires you to harness the potential of NOW CX to reimagine customer service as an essential business function that is as focused on revenue today as it has historically been on resolutions. So, let's explore how you can make this transformation in both perception and—more importantly—practice.

Zero Neglect

The leaky bucket theory of marketing suggests that, because companies are always losing customers (like water dripping from holes in a leaky bucket), they must continually acquire new customers just to maintain their existing share of the market. The better a company gets at stemming attrition (plugging the holes and stopping the leaks), the easier it becomes to grow. While this has led some to suggest that "retention is the new acquisition," as marketing author Joseph Jaffe did in his 2010 book *Flip the Funnel*, the fact is that no company can reduce the outward flow of customers to zero. That said, there's a big difference between natural ebbs and flows in buyer preferences and purchases, and the kind of neglect that sends NOW Customers rushing for the exits.

In the first part of this book, we looked at how big a problem customer neglect has become industrywide. And we calculated just how much revenue the typical ecommerce company is leaving on the table due to neglect alone—a number that could easily approach $20,000,000 per year when a single organization neglects just one digital channel. In *Part 2*, we identified the root cause of neglect (the inherent inflexibility of the legacy contact center model) and argued that modern CX departments can eradicate neglect by shifting a substantial portion of volume to a technology-enabled, on-demand expert workforce that is distributed, flexible, scalable, and always-on.

In the interest of being perfectly clear: eradicating neglect is a prerequisite for transforming customer experience into a revenue driver for your company. And embracing the human cloud is the easiest and most efficient means of eradicating neglect.

An on-demand expert workforce makes it possible to provide the rapid, responsive, efficient, and empathetic experience that NOW

Customers demand across every channel they choose, at any time around the clock, and at the high standard they expect from the world's best brands. This alone has the potential to stem the customer attrition and revenue loss that happens when a company is unavailable, inaccessible, or unable to help. In an always-on digital-by-default marketplace where 54% of ecommerce companies still don't offer after-hours support[1] and a key digital engagement channel like real-time chat is too slow, unsatisfactory, or outright unavailable 63% of the time[2], 24/7/365 omni-channel coverage can give a company a distinct advantage over its competitors. It's the kind of advantage that keeps buyers from shopping elsewhere and keeps customers coming back for more, at a time when even a 5% improvement in retention can increase profitability by anywhere from 25% to 95%.[3]

In other words, eradicating (or substantially reducing) neglect by shifting to a flexible CX staffing model plugs the holes in your bucket. So much so that your bucket might overflow. Companies with strong omni-channel customer engagement can achieve nearly three times the year-over-year revenue growth seen by companies with weaker omni-channel capabilities.[4] And the financial impact of a better customer experience is so great that, according to Forrester, a mere 1% improvement in a company's Customer Experience Index can translate to more than $1 billion in some industries.[5]

All of this said, eradicating neglect is just the tip of the iceberg. The real work of transforming CX into a revenue center involves changing the conversation. *Literally...*

Commerce Is Now Conversational

Real-time conversations have always been the foundation of customer experience, service, and support. For generations of shoppers, well-trained consultative salespeople tasked with answering questions, offering assistance, and helping customers feel confident about spending money right then and there have been the hallmark of a top-notch brick-and-mortar retail experience. And for NOW Customers, in-the-moment help and consultation as they're trying to buy online have become desirable and differentiating elements of the ecommerce shopping experience, leading them to reward the brands that offer this level of service with higher average orders and greater lifetime value. To capture the hearts, minds, and wallets of modern consumers though, your agents need to do more than just resolve issues and provide reactive responses. They must offer true convenience, convert more browsers into buyers, and drive greater customer loyalty through an approach called "conversational commerce."

Uber's Chris Messina coined the term in 2015 after noticing the ways in which voice assistants like Siri, Cortana and Amazon's new-at-the-time Alexa could handle simple shopping dialogues. As he wrote on Medium, "Conversational commerce is about delivering convenience, personalization, and decision support while people are on the go, with only partial attention to spare."[6]

Through the lens of NOW CX, Messina's focus on in-the-moment convenience and emphasis on real-time digital interactions make sense, but his vision that technology itself would be at the center of the conversation misses the mark. The definitions we offer in our own *The State of Conversational Commerce 2021* report and our other writings on the topic build on his thinking while bringing the practice closer to the proactive, decidedly human engagement a shopper would expect from a high-quality brick-and-mortar experience. Drawing on these definitions, let's think of conversational commerce in the following way:

> Conversational commerce leverages the power of dialogue to offer a personalized, consultative shopping experience that ultimately drives sales and revenue. Customer service chat and the use of messaging are critical channels for conversational commerce in the digital environment because they allow your human specialists to replicate the one-on-one, in-store

salesperson experience by enabling them to interact with customers during the buying process, provide in-the-moment help, and offer relevant recommendations while fostering relationships.

Conversational commerce forces many CX leaders to rethink the way they handle messaging (including live chat, of course, but can also include asynchronous chat and channels such as SMS)—from bot-first to human-first, from tactical to strategic, and from transactional to truly conversational. And it changes what most organizations should expect to achieve through messaging, as it becomes one key engine for transforming your CX operation from cost center to revenue driver for your company. Conversations become an avenue for delivering personalized services and product recommendations, a means of reducing customer effort by making interactions with your brand's CX team simple and helpful, and a way to leapfrog the competition's bog-standard customer service.

In a nutshell, conversational commerce turns every CX specialist into an online personal shopping assistant who knows how to turn each customer service interaction into an opportunity to add value for the buyer—while capturing value for the company, in the form of increased average order volume.

Dana Klein, who oversees ecommerce for a large footwear brand's North American region, considers this such a significant opportunity that she is "always thinking about the kind of knowledge our contact center agents need to have, so that they can better connect with the customer and even drive conversion or upsell in a brand-appropriate way."

And serial CMO and private equity executive Jeff Weiser has seen just how powerful conversational commerce can be when a company puts it into practice. "At Shutterstock, our contact center manager saw an opportunity for the care team to operate as a quasi-inside sales team. Agents could ask probing questions to understand the customer's needs more deeply, then propose other tools or solutions that would benefit them while growing their lifetime value to the company," he recounted. Jeff went on to say, "In the first year after we made this change from customer service as a cost center to customer service as a revenue driver, we quadrupled the revenue we could attribute directly to that channel. So now, we weren't just improving CSAT or Net Promoter in the hopes that satisfaction or loyalty would pay off over the long term. We could actually see the near-term impact on the bottom line."

For your own organization, consider just four common ways your CX specialists might turn the right kinds of real-time conversations into opportunities for revenue growth by:

- <u>Making Upsell Recommendations</u>. Conversational commerce can turn any service request into an opportunity to drive an incremental purchase, whether a single item naturally lends itself to add-ons or upgrades, whether full price or premium items appeal to a given buyer based upon what you learn about their preferences or know about their buying history, or whether you have items on sale, clearance, or promotion.
- <u>Suggesting Complementary Products</u>. When a customer asks about a product they're considering, ready to buy, or have already bought, proactively recommend additional items that go well with it; or make it easy for agents to suggest 'products you may like' by giving them visibility into system-based recommendations.
- <u>Providing Alternative Options</u>. When items are sold out, backordered, delayed, or otherwise unavailable, suggest comparable items the buyer may like.
- <u>Turning Returns into Exchanges</u>. Returns happen. But you can turn returns into exchanges by helping with sizing or suggesting other products they might prefer.

Ultimately, your opportunity lies in the ways you integrate conversational commerce touchpoints that align to your customers' needs at each stage of the buyer journey. When shoppers are in the earliest stage of their journey—still evaluating the widest range of alternatives that might meet their needs—agents can ask probing questions, help clarify requirements and possible solutions, build rapport, and introduce your brand and entire product portfolio in ways that encourage further consideration. As shoppers seek more *detailed* information about your brand or products and weighs these against other options, agents can provide knowledgeable recommendations. When shoppers are ready to buy, agents can reduce friction by highlighting offers, promotions, guarantees, positive reviews, and even risk-free return and exchange policies. And as shoppers reflect upon their experience after the purchase, weigh their level of satisfaction, and consider repurchase, agents can connect with them, build relationships, provide support, and reinforce favorable perceptions.

Easier Conversations Equal More Commerce

As an old saying goes, "People don't like to be sold, but they love to buy." Clearly, the point of conversational commerce is not to turn your CX specialists into shameless shills.

You may remember stories about one 2014 Comcast customer service call, during which the agent spent over an hour trying to convince *Engadget* co-founder Ryan Block and his wife not to cancel their account, even after the couple had made it clear that they were moving to a new home and had already contracted with a different provider. Block recorded the nightmarish call, which (surprise!) went viral after he posted it online, prompting an "embarrassed" Comcast to apologize for an experience a company spokeswoman acknowledged was "unacceptable and not consistent with how we train our customer service representatives."[7] As it turns out, that was exactly how they trained their reps, at least those working on the retention team, who were compensated based on their ability to reduce churn.

It should go without saying: That is *not* what we're advocating.

Done right, conversational commerce serves to reduce the level of effort required by customers to find, learn about, choose, purchase, and even enjoy products that are right for them. This matters because, according to our own research, there is a direct correlation between Customer Effort Score and likelihood to repurchase. (Just a quick heads-up that we'll be taking a detailed look at Customer Effort Score, along with a range of other NOW CX metrics, in *Chapter 9*.)

Even before getting started with conversational commerce, any steps you take to eradicate neglect will already have a positive effect on customer effort: more service hours, a wider range of channels, and seamless handoffs between bots and humans can all contribute to an easier experience. And especially for pre-sale interactions, the very fact that you provide access to human agents can have a notable effect on effort. Shoppers in our *2021 State of Conversational Commerce* study found that their interactions with human agents tended to be "easy," while their chatbot conversations (without human agent intervention) were more likely to be "difficult."[8]

This tells us that there is a clear correlation between human-centered messaging and the ease of the customer's interaction with the brand. And when a brand incorporates conversational commerce approaches into those human-centered messages to make it easier for customers to find the right products, get answers to questions, and make purchases, the better the results are for the business. In fact, we saw a direct relationship between positive customer effort score and the likelihood of repurchase: shoppers who rated their level of effort "very easy" were nearly three times as likely to say they'd buy again than shoppers who rated effort "very difficult."[9]

And consumer repurchase intent when human agents were involved reached 88%, while repurchase intent based on chat experiences with no human help was a relatively paltry 11%.[10]

CUSTOMER EFFORT SCORE

In other words, the more your customers love buying from you, the more likely they'll be to buy from you again and again. And the better your agents become at turning rapport and recommendations into revenue, the more likely you'll be to break away from the perception that customer service is just sunk cost.

Even if this sounds great in theory, you might still be wondering how CX organizations make conversations pay off in practice.

Real Talk

In much the same way that the human cloud and machine cloud work together to allow for the deployment of a flexible and scalable CX capability, an effective combination of humans and technology underpin conversational commerce.

As we've already seen, consultative selling in practice calls for a greater level of nuance and know-how than you can expect from a bot. That's why human specialists are uniquely suited for conversational commerce. But without a certain amount of digital assistance and good visibility into relevant customer and product data, your agents may not be fully equipped to carry on the right conversations.

For this, it's vital that any agent tasked with commerce in their conversations have access to the just-in-time information they'll need, in a simple user-friendly platform that ties directly into your customer data repository, ecommerce platform, inventory management system, and shopping cart software (not to mention your ticketing and other customer support systems). In practice, we're talking about a system that can proactively present the agent with contextually relevant personal and commercial "connection prompts" that will allow them to naturally move any given conversation toward easier engagement and a more satisfying (not to mention, profitable) purchasing experience. In fact, by providing this kind of enabling technology through the cloud for both internal employees and external on-demand agents creates consistency between these two portions of your hybrid customer care workforce, allowing both teams to be equally effective in executing your conversational commerce plan.

Let's consider just a few of the possible scenarios you might unlock with the right combination of empowered humans and enabling technology.

- The Upsell. Kim has three shirts in her shopping cart when she connects with a human agent to be sure about sizing. The rep addresses Kim's immediate need: all three tops run true-to-size. In the process, she sees that one of the three items is among her own personal favorites; it's a product she owns and wears herself and she immediately suggests a pair of shorts that complements it well. Kim agrees that they're a great match for the shirt she's about to buy and adds it to her cart, resulting in a larger order size.

- <u>The Rescue</u>. Andrew is shopping for a luggage set for an upcoming family vacation. While on the product page, he engages in an automated chat to get a sense of shipping speed and costs but is still concerned that his family's new suitcases may not arrive in time for their travel. He requests a hand-off to a human agent who comes into the chat armed with all the information Andrew has already shared with the bot (nobody likes to repeat the same information, so a seamless transfer is important), knowledge of which product Andrew is considering, and awareness that Andrew's concern over shipping times might drive him to Amazon for Prime two-day turnaround. Seeing that Andrew is a new customer, the agent recognizes an opportunity to make a great first impression. The agent recommends an alternative luggage set with similar specs, fantastic customer reviews, and immediate availability. He offers to upgrade Andrew's order to the fastest shipping option at no additional cost, to ensure it arrives on time, locking in what could be the first of many orders over the course of this new customer's lifetime.

- <u>The Loyalty Play</u>. Cara purchased some newborn products almost a full year ago and is shopping the company's site for the first time since then. During a pre-sale customer service chat, the agent proactively recommends a cartload of bestselling age-appropriate items for Cara's daughter who will be turning one next month. The agent also offers to add Cara to the company's age-by-age parenting tips newsletter, which will keep her informed about upcoming childrearing milestones, new products, and promotions—helping to keep the brand top-of-mind and to convert Cara from occasional browser to frequent buyer.

With scenarios like these, it becomes clear that conversational commerce can deliver more value and drive more revenue than customer service is traditionally given credit for. But turning CX into a revenue driver doesn't need to end there.

So Good They'll Pay for It

Conversational commerce is a natural evolution of a human-first, technology-enabled customer experience. It leverages the same two core components you've put in place to offer an around-the-clock omni-channel model for engagement: a top-notch network of on-demand experts and enabling technologies accessible from anywhere through the cloud. It expands the notion of service, moving it beyond rapid resolutions to relevant recommendations and making online shopping more familiar and friendly—not to mention more efficient and easier—in a world that has become increasingly digital. But there are certainly additional ways to turn a profit through premium service and support—including one that takes a page out of the Amazon Prime playbook. We're talking about *service-as-a-product*.

Amazon Prime, with its $119 annual fee, has shown that NOW Customers are willing to pay for the benefits that come with premium service. So much so that NOW companies like DoorDash, Lyft, and Instacart all offer premium service upgrades for a fee. DashPass, Lyft Pink, and Instacart Express (respectively) all cost more upfront, commit customers to annual contracts, and offer benefits that range from savings *over time* to preferred treatment. The concept is hardly new, and even traditional retailers have proven that consumers will spend more for stand-apart service.

Take Geek Squad, for example. Best Buy acquired the little-known computer repair service in 2002, after struggling to gain a foothold with maintenance contracts for the machines it sold in its stores. In the decade that followed, Geek Squad—which unlike the Apple Genius Bar charges fees for its technical support services—grew into "a cash cow for Best Buy," with industry analysts estimating that the service arm of the big box retailer was generating "a gross profit margin of 40 to 50 percent based on a minimum annual revenue of $2 billion."[11]

Since that time, Geek Squad has been operating under an even broader remit with an even larger potential market: subscription-based installation, setup, support, and repair services for just about any electronic device, purchased from any seller. Services are offered in-store, on-location, and through 24/7 phone and online channels. As one tech reporter noted when Best Buy announced these expanded service options, "They install GPS devices on cars. They lead in-store smartphone tutorials for customers. They advise homeowners on how to reduce energy bills. They tell hospitals how to safely transmit patient records through tablets."[12] In other words, they're in front of customers, offering sophisticated consultation that—as Best Buy senior vice president Josh Will notes—helps buyers make the most of their technology purchases, and pays out for the company "in customer loyalty and customer satisfaction."[13] But it pays out in other important ways too: Geek Squad remains a high margin service, played a vital role in the company's pre-pandemic turnaround strategy, and remains a notable source of revenue for the electronics giant today.

Ask yourself: Could NOW CX enable your organization to offer a consultative experience so good your customers would be willing to pay for it as a productized service?

And while we're on the topic of questions, let's return to the question Phil Libin posed to Shannon Jimenez at the start of this chapter. How can a CX leader champion the support team and convince the rest of the organization (especially the executive team) that customer experience shouldn't be seen as a cost center anymore?

Selling Your Ability to Sell to the C-Suite

Even a few short years ago—before *every* customer became a NOW Customer, and certainly before the pandemic accelerated ecommerce adoption and changed consumer expectations across the board—many otherwise reasonable corporate executives might have argued that bad customer service was good for business. *Heresy!* But this is exactly what Anthony Dukes and Yi Zhu, two business school marketing professors, contend in a 2019 *Harvard Business Review* article. Citing a variety of studies spanning the 2010s and supported by several years of their own firsthand research into why companies make service so hard for their customers, Dukes and Zhu conclude that "some companies may actually find it profitable to create hassles for complaining customers," that "companies with few competitors [in particular] may find it worthwhile to alienate angry customers in order to save on redress costs," and that "this may help us understand why some of the most hated companies in America are so profitable and why customer service, unfortunately, remains so frustrating."[14]

While it would take a particularly staunch defender of the status quo to make this same argument *today*, the fact remains that many C-suite leaders harbor a rather old school mindset when it comes to customer care. This alone could explain the prevalence of business leaders outside of CX who love the idea of customer centricity in theory but resist efforts (and investments) that would make their company more customer centric in practice. Sure, they *want* buyers to have a good experience with the company. They *want* the brand to benefit from more consumer love, loyalty, and advocacy. But when faced with the prospect of investing significantly to upgrade the experience, they're bound to question the return on their investment. After all, what's the upside of efficiency? Where's the net profit in Net Promoter? What's the direct relationship between satisfaction and shareholder value?

Clearly, you can't answer questions like these with a shoulder shrug or a litany of soft benefits that fall short of bolstering the bottom line. Sure, you're making the leap from cost center to revenue driver by eradicating neglect and committing to conversational commerce or other revenue-generating service models. But now, you'll need to *prove* the work is paying off—by presenting a strong economic argument, framed in the language of the C-suite, and supported with the right performance metrics.

To help you make your case, *Chapter 9* is all about the new metrics—from Customer Effort Score to customer lifetime value—you can use to measure the performance of your revenue-oriented customer service operation and show the rest of your organization why NOW CX is a smart investment.

CHAPTER 9

Why You Need to Rethink Your Customer Experience KPIs

Is Efficiency the Enemy of Excellence?

At this point, it seems safe to say that we're all on the same page about eradicating customer neglect and transforming CX into a revenue center. These are game-changing steps to delivering on the promise of NOW CX, and making these moves can elevate your service experience for customers and contribute to stronger results for your business.

But as we elevate the practice of CX, shouldn't we also elevate the way we track and report on it? Put another way, why would we measure NOW CX practices with legacy metrics?

The truth is that some of the most common CX metrics in use today are out of sync with a NOW CX approach. A former call center executive (who—unsurprisingly—asked not to be named) spoke with us and exposed some hard truths about efficiency metrics' reign over traditional customer service:

"At the end of the day, efficiency is still the most important umbrella metric at most call centers. And this cuts across everything. For email, it's usually how many emails somebody can answer in a shift, which is basically measuring productivity. When you get into chat, handle time still ends up being important, along with concurrency (how many chats can agents have at once), so that's still about volume and efficiency. It's even embedded into training. When I ran training in a call center, the number one metric I was held accountable for was how many weeks it took for someone in my program to match the average handle time of the agents already on the floor. If you were a fly on the wall in a typical contact center, you'd think that minimizing handle time is the only thing that matters."

We're not saying you shouldn't measure the basics at all, but we do think it's important to consider whether volume and efficiency metrics are meaningful in the age of experience. The hard truth here is that when contact centers focus purely on minimizing handle times, they're prioritizing productivity over satisfaction and efficiency over experience.

CX industry expert Nicole France has some strong thoughts about this, and her views may feel like a bombshell in a traditional contact center setting:

"I actually think efficiency is one of the problems with the legacy contact center model that is holding CX back. 'How many calls were answered in this hour?' 'How many emails were responded to?' Whereas, if you viewed each CX interaction as an opportunity to build a relationship with a customer, you'd be more focused on the quality of conversation, not just the length of it."

It should come as no surprise that we agree. Think about it: By whipping through service interactions to maximize efficiency, agents (and bots) are undoubtedly missing chances to have the types of conversations that reveal opportunities to strengthen customer ties with the business, capture more sales, and increase revenue. Remember that conversational commerce stuff we talked about in *Chapter 8?* Without an emphasis on making space for conversation, the commerce part will undoubtedly suffer.

NOW CX isn't about speed alone; it's about meeting customers in their 'now' to deliver the right kind of experience at the right moment. NOW Customers expect excellent service, and with a NOW CX mindset, we know that excellence has to trump efficiency.

An Alphabet Soup of CX Metrics

Although efficiency metrics may still rule the day within traditional contact centers, many CX teams are using a variety of additional metrics to help measure effectiveness and success. This certainly moves CX in the right direction, but many alphabet soups of metrics still aren't *quite* enough when customer service departments are trying to shake the cost center stigma and move into a more strategic and revenue-centric position in the organization.

In this section, we'll cover a variety of CX metrics that together can illustrate your effectiveness in a NOW CX environment.

Now, if you feel that you've already mastered all of these metrics, you can treat this section as a "choose your own CX adventure" and skip ahead to the next part. Otherwise, stick with us as we dive into a discussion of the metrics NOW CX leaders need to track.

Satisfaction-Based Metrics

Customer Satisfaction Score (CSAT)

Customer Satisfaction Scores are gathered through surveys and questionnaires to help companies understand how satisfied customers are with their business. The key aspects measured in customer satisfaction are what customers think about your brand, products or services, and experience with your customer service team or resources. The primary purpose of customer satisfaction surveys is to determine customers who are pleased with your business, those who are displeased, and why. You may have seen your company's own CSAT score expressed as a percentage that was calculated by dividing all the positive responses by the total number of responses and multiplying by 100—or as an average score, such as the way a Lyft driver might be rated at 4.89 stars out of 5.

However, CSAT is just the tip of the iceberg in terms of measuring NOW Customers and how they feel about your business and CX. In fact, for every CSAT survey response you get back, there will be lots of customers who aren't raising their hand to provide feedback. Savvy CX leaders know that low response rates on CSAT surveys can, in and of themselves, point to lingering, undiagnosed experience issues and can be a sure sign that your customers don't care enough to let you know where you stand. In short, customer neglect often festers among the pool of participants who couldn't be bothered to respond.

So, while CSAT might be a decent indicator of where you're doing well and where you need to improve, it certainly doesn't tell the complete story of how your company is performing as a whole.

Net Promoter Score (NPS)

Net Promoter Score is a metric that helps to gauge customer satisfaction and loyalty by asking your customers if they would recommend your business to friends, relatives, or colleagues based on the quality of the experience you deliver.

Your NPS is a number that represents the percentage of your customers who are most likely to recommend your business to a friend on a scale of 0 to 10. NPS survey respondents then fall into one of three categories: Detractors (those who give a 0-6 rating), Passives (those who give a 7-8 rating), or Promoters (those who give a 9-10 rating). The Net Promoter Score is calculated as the difference between the percentage of promoters and detractors.

Let's explore the three NPS result categories:

- Detractors (0-6 score)
  The customers who give ratings within this range are displeased with your company or CX, and you should not expect word-of-mouth referrals from them. On the flip side, they might even damage your brand through negative reviews, posts, and conversations.
- Passives (7-8 score)
  Customers who give ratings between 7 and 8 are those who rate your business as "satisfactory," but are generally unenthusiastic buyers or subscribers. These lukewarm customers could be swayed by a competitor's slightly better price, discount, shipping speed, or other benefits. Passives will not damage your brand like Detractors, so they are not typically included in the NPS calculation.
- Promoters (9-10 score)
  Customers who give a 9 or 10 rating are your biggest fans and your most enthusiastic brand advocates. These customers will eagerly promote your brand to family and friends. They could help you increase market share from your competitors by sharing positive messages and experiences with family, friends, or followers. In most cases, Promoters are your loyal and repeat customers, so it's essential that you put in the effort to expand this group.

Now, we should point out here that there are actually two ways to measure (and understand) NPS—one that focuses on a point in time and one that is more focused on loyalty over time. The first, Transactional NPS, often produces higher ratings based on surveys sent in conjunction with a specific transaction or interaction, capturing sentiment while the consumer is still "high from the buy." For this reason, Transactional NPS scores may be a less meaningful measure of loyalty over time. Relationship NPS, on the other hand, uses surveys sent on a regular basis and not in conjunction with a purchase. Response rates and the resulting scores tend to be lower (compared to their Transactional scores) for most companies, but are a far more meaningful measure of true customer loyalty.

Since NPS—and especially Relationship NPS—provides a window into customer loyalty, it can help create an actionable plan to drive better customer reviews and increased revenue through referral marketing. NPS, in conjunction with other key metrics, can play an important role in painting a picture of your CX effectiveness.

Effort-Focused Metrics

Customer Effort Score (CES)

Customer Effort Score is a CX metric that explores the ease of doing business with your brand. CES measures how much effort (see also: frustration, aggravation, *neglect*) a customer has to go through when they interact with your business. By asking customers about their experience through the lens of effort, you can better understand just how easy (or not) it is for a customer to make a purchase or troubleshoot a problem. RBI's Jake Lechnir agrees, sharing that "one of the metrics that has become increasingly important is Customer Effort Score, which I think can be pretty highly correlated to brand loyalty." This should come as no surprise considering that, according to a November 19 blog post by Gartner, 94% of customers with low-effort interactions intend to purchase again, compared with a mere 4% of those experiencing high effort.

Typically deployed as a one-question survey, CES is calculated by dividing the sum of all individual customer effort scores by the number of customers who provided a response. The higher your CES, the better the overall average experience across all your customers. In one method, the rating could vary from "very diffi-cult" to "very easy" when asked to rate their ease of finding products or completing a transaction. In another, customers might be asked about the extent to which they agree that a company made it easy to resolve their issue, with CES representing the percentage who gave the company a five or better ("somewhat agree" or higher).

In either scenario, CES is an important metric in NOW CX because high-effort experiences negatively impact customer loyalty and other revenue- and value-centric measures. By measuring effort through a CES survey, CX leaders can identify at-risk customers, proactively reach out to them, and remove obstacles for the cus-tomer to reduce customer service costs and attrition rates. By follow-ing up on the results of a CES survey, CX teams can more quickly and effectively address issues that may stand in the way of revenue generation and customer loyalty. Using CES data in combination with NPS and CSAT data can help CX teams to improve customer experience, increase loyalty, and support revenue growth.

Site Conversion Rate (CVR)

Site conversion rate is defined as the percentage of your website visitors that complete a "desired action" out of the total number of visitors. Now, what that "desired action" is might vary depending on your industry. For many retail and ecommerce companies, you'd most likely track the percent of shoppers who become buyers by making an online purchase during their visit to your site. In indus-tries with more complex sales cycles—let's say business software-as-a-service—you might calculate CVR based on whether or not a visitor books a demo, requests a quote, registers for an upcoming virtual event, or even consumes a key piece of product content. And for companies that do most of their business in the physical world—say, a quick service restaurant or automotive dealer—you might monitor the portion of visitors who use your online store locator, request a quote, or download a printable coupon.

No matter what industry you're in though, you want to have a high CVR, as it translates to more inquiries, purchases, and overall revenue. At the same time, CVR can give insight into customer effort; if people are having trouble navigating your site, accessing support, and making a purchase, you'll likely see your CVR dip.

In terms of acceptable CVRs, industry averages tend to hover around 2.4%, while top performers can convert at 10% or more. A CVR below 3.5% should prompt you to reevaluate your site immediately, particularly if you're running an ecommerce store. Remember: a higher CVR typically indicates stronger sales, and tying CX to sales growth goes a long way in proving that customer experience is a revenue driver, not a cost center.

Revenue-Centric Metrics

Value Enhancement Score (VES)

Value Enhancement Score, a CX metric created by Gartner, enables businesses to measure the value that customers place on a product or service. While CSAT and NPS are adept at predicting attitudinal loyalty (e.g. what customers say they *will* or *would* do), they fall short of illustrating behavioral loyalty (i.e. what customers *actually did*). And that's where VES comes in.

VES is calculated through a two-question, post-transaction survey in which the customer rates their agreement with the following statements on a scale of 1 (strongly disagree) through 7 (strongly agree):

- After the customer service interaction, I am able to achieve more with the product.
- After the customer service interaction, my confidence in my decision to purchase the product is higher.

As an indicator of the customer's confidence in the decision to buy from you, VES is a leading predictor of customer loyalty across all key dimensions—customer retention, increased wallet share, and positive word-of-mouth. In fact, through the research Gartner conducted that led to the development of the VES metric, they found that customers who feel they have received positive value during a service interaction are 86% more likely to increase their wallet share with that company or brand.[1]

And as Devin Poole, Senior Director, Advisory, at Gartner wrote in an article on value enhancement score, "Shifting from CSAT and NPS to the VES will allow CSS [customer service and support] leaders to demonstrate their ability to drive revenue."[2] And that's the name of the game, folks.

Repurchase Rate (RR)

Repurchase rate is the percentage of your customers who make another order or buy another product or service from you within a given time frame. RR indicates how many customers are returning to you to buy again, which helps to show you how well your offerings and CX are meeting the wants and needs of your market.

The time frame for calculating RR usually falls along a 30-, 60-, 90-, 180-, or 360-day period, although some time ranges might be longer. For example, if 60 out of 250 customers who placed an order in September place another order within the next 30 days, your RR would be 24%.

The span of time for measuring your RR should be chosen to align with the type and rhythm of your business. Think about it: the repurchase rate for major appliances will naturally follow a different timeline than repurchase rates for toothpaste. *Or at least we'd hope it does.*

Repurchase rate is a revenue-centric metric that CX teams should not overlook, especially because customer service often plays a role in why some people choose to buy again—*or not.* Jake Lechnir nailed it when he told us, "If you combine high guest satisfaction to begin with and low effort when a guest does need support, you're going to see an increase in repeat purchases. I think having this kind of insight gives companies one way to demonstrate ROI and prove that customer service is a channel that can do more than collect feedback and address issues; it can improve brand loyalty and increase revenue."

Customer Lifetime Value (CLV)

Customer lifetime value indicates the profit your company or brand can expect to generate from an individual customer throughout the course of your relationship with that customer. And the longer a customer keeps purchasing from you, the greater their CLV becomes.

To measure your overall CLV, you need to look at the average margin earned per purchase for a typical customer, then multiply by the average number of purchases in a typical year. Once you arrive at that number, you multiply by the average customer lifespan with your business (in other words, the average retention time in number of years) to arrive at your CLV.

You can also run the CLV calculation for specific customers or customer segments to see where you are excelling or falling short. Where you have strong CLV results, you can do more of what's working to increase those customers' happiness and loyalty, and where you have weak CLV results, you can troubleshoot and then use NOW CX tactics to improve the experience in ways that raise your score.

Beware of the Metrics Manipulators

As business leaders, we tend to rely on quantifiable metrics because— as the old adage goes— "numbers don't lie." Except, of course, when they do.

Many of us have learned the hard way that you can't always take the data coming from various teams at face value. Individual employees, teams, and technology vendors often want to tell the best possible story about their programs, and some will have no problem manipulating the metrics to help them tell that story. OK, so maybe numbers don't lie, but people do. And when it comes to CX programs, it's no different.

Here are some real examples of how the KPIs above can be manipulated:

- In order to maintain a good CSAT score, a customer service agent may grant an exception to a customer, like a full refund, when they're not supposed to. The customer will be satisfied, but the company unexpectedly loses money.

- Some organizations will only report first response times during normal business hours. This paints an inaccurate portrait of how well the team is performing in terms of responding to customers. More importantly, it can give support organizations a pass for ignoring customers during off-hours.

- Many ticketing systems will automatically suppress the distribution of measurement tools like NPS surveys during certain circumstances (overnight, when certain macros and processes are being used, and so on). Customer service agents who have provided a poor experience to a customer will wait to resolve a ticket for that inquiry until those circumstances are met, meaning the customer never receives an NPS score and therefore can't express their dissatisfaction.

- Chatbot providers can artificially inflate the deflection rates they report to their customers. One common practice among chatbot providers is to proactively surface only the types of inquiries that it can handle to a consumer engaged in a chat. For example, a bot might limit the consumer's options to avoid the number of unresolved interactions it escalates. For example: a bot might ask, "What can I help you with today? Then offer just a few possible replies: "[Request a refund] [Where is my order?] [Edit my order]." Particularly in pre-sales situations, a consumer may try once or twice to find an answer to a question that exists outside the limited options offered by the chatbot. Then, they'll simply shop elsewhere. Meanwhile, the chatbot does not include this as a missed deflection; the inquiry is simply never registered at all.

Because of scenarios like these, we recommend implementing robust and stringent audit and quality/accuracy assurance protocols to ensure that the numbers that CX teams report out reflect the real story of how customers are interacting with your brand. For example, at Simplr we audit 15% of inquiries from our specialists (industry averages range between two and five percent). Each audited ticket receives one of three possible scores:

1. "Positive" means the ticket was handled flawlessly and nothing at all could've been reasonably improved.
2. "Neutral" means that ultimately the right answer was given but could've been improved in some small way (too much unnecessary back-and-forth to get the right answer, or perhaps not enough empathy was shown for the customer's situation).
3. "Negative" ratings are reserved for defects where the policies, processes, or tone are not followed.

The data that comes from our audits is invaluable in terms of further improving our specialists' behavior and guaranteeing an excellent customer experience time in and time out.

Measuring CX Success in Your Business's Language

When we said there was an alphabet soup of CX metrics, we were only kind of kidding. Clearly there are a plethora of ways CX teams can measure their activities and effectiveness, ranging from satisfaction-based metrics to effort-focused metrics and through to revenue-centric metrics.

While it may be tempting to stick to the CSAT and NPS measures that feel familiar, if you want your CX function to operate as and be perceived as a revenue center in your organization, you will need to measure against and communicate with metrics that speak the language of your business. And that ultimately comes down to finding a blend of measures that align with your business's goals and your executives' objectives.

Furthering a NOW CX environment requires a better understanding of how CX is contributing to the overall health of your business, and the way you measure and prove that value will set up CX for a move into a central strategic role in the company. For more on CX's meteoric rise as a driver of business strategy, turn the page to *Chapter 10*.

CHAPTER 10

Why CX Should Be Driving Your Business Strategy

Experience Really Is Everything

Dana Klein doesn't have the words *customer experience* on her business card, but she certainly has them in her job description, at the top of her mind, and on the tip of her tongue. And as the GM Digital, North America for a global footwear brand, Dana's definition of CX extends well beyond the confines of the contact center. "My team is responsible for the *entire* experience," she told us. "This starts from the moment a consumer sees a first piece of marketing and continues through the whole product lifecycle—looking for new points of engagement and interaction."

Such a broad perspective shouldn't surprise anyone who has watched the emergence and elevation of customer experience as a business concept over the course of the past decade and a half. In their seminal 2007 *Harvard Business Review* article on the subject, Andre Schwager and Chris Meyer wrote, "Customer experience encompasses every aspect of a company's offering—the quality of customer care, of course, but also advertising, packaging, product and service features, ease of use, and reliability."[1]

By this standard, CX doesn't just support the business; it *is* the business. By 2015, Gartner had declared "customer experience the new battlefield" after finding that 89% of companies said that CX—not product features, innovation, or even quality of service alone—would be their primary basis for competition.[2] Given this, it should come as no surprise that in 2021 the vast majority of companies have a chief experience officer, chief customer officer, or—at a minimum—another senior leader responsible for how the brand engages with its buyers.

For all practical purposes, Dana Klein functions as her company's CXO—for the North American region at least—regardless of the title on her business card. You may find yourself in a similar role. You may even *be* a chief experience officer or chief customer officer at your company. If not, the odds are good that you report to someone who holds the title or fills the role.

While none of this guarantees that the senior-most CX person in *your* organization has the CEO's ear or even a seat in the C-suite, it does imply that customer experience has a champion to carry the torch. So, why does it seem like customer service still isn't as central to your company's value proposition as it should be? And how can it be that the rest of the executive team still gives customer experience more lip service than serious consideration? And how can you elevate the role of CX, position yourself as a strategic partner to the C-suite, and turn your relationships with customers into a source of strategic value?

We've already taken you through the essential work of eradicating neglect, turning customer service into a revenue center, and demonstrating your worth with a more robust set of KPIs. Now, let's look at three levers for making NOW CX an indispensable strategic driver for the entire company:

- <u>Master the Matrix</u>: Yielding Influence Over CX Across the Organization
- <u>Keep Better Company</u>: Aligning and Integrating with Other Revenue Drivers
- <u>Be Data-Driven</u>: Leveraging Customer Data and Insights for Decision-Making

Master the Matrix

Even though nearly all organizations have named a customer experience czar, Gartner's research seems to suggest that the implementation of siloed CX projects and programs remains scattered throughout a typical company in departments as diverse as sales, marketing, operations, IT, and of course customer service. Indeed, their 2019 *Customer Experience Management Study* cast a wide net, surveying personnel across all of these functional areas to gain a comprehensive view of the state of CX.[3] If this in fact the way CX programs are managed today, then the situation hasn't improved much in the 14 years since Schwager and Meyer lamented that "few of the people responsible for those things have given sustained thought to how their separate decisions shape customer experience. To the extent they do think about it, they all have different ideas of what customer experience means, and no one more senior oversees everyone's efforts."[4]

Centralizing all aspects of customer experience—the strategy, design, funding, and management—under a single top-level executive would seem to be the obvious fix. As executive staffing firm MarketPro notes, "Having one go-to executive with the knowledge and authority to modify and calibrate the entire [CX] process makes it much easier to deliver a cohesive experience."[5] And user experience consultant Carola Fellenz Thomspon validates this based on her personal experience as the former chief experience officer at security management company Splunk: "A well-built and managed experience team with executive authority offers a new kind of nimbleness that makes creating an organization-wide experience compelling and responsive."[6]

In some companies—particularly those with a C-level customer experience leader—this may be exactly how things work. In others though, it's important for the person in charge of customer service and support to achieve a position of influence (if not authority) with peers who might oversee important CX initiatives but who may not share your same focus on true customer-centricity. The notion of *influence-without-authority* is hardly new. Many organizations have been matrixed for quite a while, with dotted lines on the organizational chart and indirect reporting structures in practice overshadowing formal lines of command.

As one article on the Harvard Business School blog points out, "Someone who works in their organization's accounting or finance department can hold incredible influence over a project during the budgeting and planning phase when resources are being allocated. Similarly, human resources—as gatekeepers during the hiring process—can hold a tremendous amount of influence and sway over a range of projects and departments due to their role."[7] Neither scenario should feel foreign to any CX leader, who knows from experience just how much control the finance department has over your contact center budget and how it impacts your resource plan when your in-house recruiters deprioritize your open headcount.

While those are negative examples, there are obvious benefits to attaining a position of influence inside an organization. For CX professionals, the advantage derives from being a strategic partner to peers and delivers an increased sense of customer-centricity that infuses CX-related projects (wherever they're managed in the company) and ultimately shapes strategic decisions made everywhere in the organization.

On one level, influence is a function of the strong, mutually beneficial relationships you build with executives in other parts of the business. On another, influence is earned by the level of subject matter expertise you bring to those relationships. For a customer service professional, expertise comes not merely from being an expert in service but from being an expert in the customer. In an organization without a chief experience officer who wields direct authority over all elements of end-to-end CX, you can earn and exert your influence in strategic conversations by becoming a champion for the customer and an expert in everything that affects the customer's relationship with the company. Ideally, the expertise you bring to the table or build over time includes:

- Mapping the end-to-end customer journey
- Attaining a robust understanding of the customer's pains, gains, jobs-to-do, and motivations; then educating the rest of the company about the customer
- Identifying experiential gaps and engagement opportunities to better serve the customer at every stage of their journey
- Designing and delivering experiences to customers through omni-channel customer service (and beyond)
- Implementing revenue-oriented approaches like conversational commerce as a means of increasing lifetime value and loyalty
- Creating connections between CX and employee experience (given the link between the two) and advocating for the integration they require
- Championing customers' perspectives in the company's strategic decision-making
- Measuring the impact of CX on employees, the impact of EX on customers, and the impact of both on the company's KPIs

In short, your value as a strategic driver increases as you gain the understanding you need to garner the influence you'll need to shape the way peers and leaders in your organization think about and serve the customer. But this alone is not enough. For CX to move into the strategic center of the business, customer experience must better align—even integrate—with the company's other key revenue driving functions.

Keep Better Company (in Your Company)

Certainly, an effective CXO will have deep relationships with their executive team peers, forging strong ties with the CTO, CIO, CMO, CFO, and even CEO. But we're talking about something a bit different here—how companies can better align and best structure their teams for stronger customer-centricity and greater CX success.

Historically, the marketing and customer experience functions focus their energies on opposite sides of the pre/post-sale divide. As Forrester notes in *The Future of Customer Insights Will Power Next Best Experiences*, "Unfortunately, in most businesses, marketers focus on the initial stages of the customer lifecycle and CX pros focus on the later stages. [Even though] in reality, journeys often collide, exist in parallel, or are interdependent."[8] This disconnect causes the customer's experience with the company to fracture along departmental lines—which is problematic, given that the typical customer doesn't know (or frankly, care) how you're organized internally, why certain decisions are "out of your hands," or why things that seem simple can be impossibly complex. To the customer, the brand is the brand—a single, unified entity that owes them a consistent and holistic experience that puts the brand promise into CX practice.

Dana Klein has seen this disconnected dynamic firsthand and understands its effects. As she described in our conversation, "At the end of the day, the customer journey is whatever the consumer decides it's going to be. And as a company, it's our job to be present all along that journey, to be consistent at every point on that journey, and to engage one-on-one with the consumer as a person. That can't happen if—for example—performance marketing is separate from brand management, brand never talks to the channel, your ecommerce store is part of a standalone business unit, and customer service rolls up to a totally different part of the business."

This explains, in part, why these otherwise disparate functions all roll up to Dana as part of a single integrated North American digital business unit that owns the end-to-end experience it offers its online customers. And it suggests that one approach for making CX a strategic driver at any organization lies in the combination of customer service with other revenue-generating functions into a single unit that owns the end-to-end experience. In an organization without a C-level customer experience leader today, it might mean making the decision to move customer service into an existing revenue-oriented department like customer success, ecommerce, or marketing.

In fact, marketing might be a particularly apt home for customer service. This would certainly help erase the organizational divide between the early and late stages of the customer lifecycle. And it would also play into a possible shift in where an increasing amount of CX authority lies in many organizations.

Gartner has found that chief marketing officers are exerting more and more control over CX, even in organizations that have a chief experience or chief customer officer. And that those CXOs and CCOs are unlikely to be part of marketing's chain of command. Gartner VP analyst Augie Ray notes, "These roles rarely report to CMOs despite marketing taking control of more CX initiatives."[9] This, even though many CXOs are likely to be marketers themselves. As global staffing firm Robert Half explains in their online profile of the position, "A strong marketing background is a must," along with "experience across various digital marketing channels... [and] depending on the industry a background in more traditional advertising methods."[10] Whether your CXO is a trained marketer and even if your organization has not yet appointed a CXO, combining marketing and customer experience in a single department or business unit—overseen by a single authoritative and influential executive—may be the answer to instilling customer-centricity at the core of your company.

Having said this, we do want to be clear. There is no single solution that will work everywhere. Every organization is different, and the dynamics of your business will determine where your CX team should report. In fact, it's reasonable and realistic for CX to remain a standalone department, as long as it is strategically aligned with other revenue centers, around the shared priorities of customer loyalty and lifetime value. And as long as the mechanisms exist to foster cross-functional collaboration around the wants and needs of the customer.

In *The Future of Customer Insights Will Power Next Best Experiences*, Forrester shares an example of this in action. The report, authored by analyst Brandon Purcell, states, "To avoid 'journey bias,' brands must assign a cross-functional team consisting of a business sponsor, a journey owner, and design and delivery partners to optimize a specific journey. Bank of Montreal successfully did this when it formed cross-functional agile teams to align focus around key journeys that matter, as well as a Customer Optimization Forum to prioritize the key conversations that the company wants to have with its customers across channels."[11]

"I don't think there's only one structure that can work, but I think the company culture should always be oriented towards making the customer happy," says investor and serial CMO Jeff Weiser. "I was working with a company recently that told me that when there's a complaint the only guardrails on their service team are designed to make the customer happy immediately. They don't care how you do it. They don't care what it costs. It's too short a game to do anything else. That mindset and culture is more important than whether you organize customer care with marketing or ecommerce or operations for that matter."

To us, this sounds like the right formula for reducing customer effort and eradicating neglect. It's the kind of thinking (and doing) that separates revenue drivers from cost centers, earns repeat transactions, inspires customer loyalty, and increases lifetime value.

Now, let's move from the "soft" stuff of influence, authority, alignment, and culture to the role hard data plays in moving CX into the strategic center of the business.

Be Data-Driven

According to Forrester's recent report, *The State of Customer Analytics 2020*, "This year, over half of companies said they're applying customer analytics to product development and pricing decisions."[12]

RBI's Jake Lechnir says, "Customer service interactions can provide companies with an incredible source of feedback data that can be used to drive incremental improvements for their business." For starters, this means that even an isolated customer complaint might serve as an early warning system, a flag that there is a more widespread issue—whether in a digital channel, a physical location, with a promotion, or with a product—that a company can address proactively and preemptively before it impacts a larger portion of its customer base. We think of this as "proactive issue avoidance." In other words, solving challenges even before your customers know they exist by identifying and operationalizing fixes to the underlying causes of buyer friction, customer complaints, and even neglect.

If we look beyond data as a means of improving quality of service, we can see that the strategic application of customer insights beyond CX creates a scenario in which the voice of the customer might ultimately factor into a wide array of product and service decisions. This could mean optimizing your brands' preferences and needs. Even needs that are unexpressed but can be inferred from the rich trail of digital data customers leave as they interact with your company's digital support channels.

It's no surprise that, in a world where interactions are increasingly digital and data is more plentiful than ever before, Forrester notes that these advanced, consumer-centric applications of customer analytics "should continue to be growth areas for customer analytics, especially as more companies develop connected products and adopt dynamic pricing in the future."[13]

This is a growth area for CX leaders as well. The more important customer insights become to the business overall—and the better the customer service team becomes at capturing and channeling those insights to the people who can use them for strategic decision-making—the more central the customer experience function becomes to the company.

Alexandra Vidaeff, director of client services at FRAME, shares this vision. While in her prior role leading customer experience at fashion brand ANINE BING, she welcomed the opportunity it created for the CX professionals on her team and saw the potential it held for building even stronger bonds between the brand and the women who buy from it. "We weren't quite at the center of the company just yet, but we *were* feeding a lot of really good information to the channels to improve business processes," Alex told us. "We were also working to create a feedback system so that we can get the right information to the right people." Looking ahead to the future of customer experience as a strategic driver for entire enterprises, Alex says:

> "I would really like to see CX at the core of the entire company. So, any time a major decision is made, nothing is decided until the decision makers hear from the customer service team. Real customer data could shape new marketing initiatives, upgrades to programs we already offer and the launch of new programs,

even new designs or design modifications. We should be the first place that people across the company come for insights. We have a direct line to our customers. So, coming to customer service is like going directly to the customer herself—and nothing happens without hearing from the customer first."

"For this to work," Lechnir adds, "You need to have a shared philosophy across teams, and multiple people bought into the idea of leveraging customer service data to improve the business."

Taking this further, cultivating a shared philosophy of customer-centricity and then acting on customer service data to improve the business is a strategic imperative for any company that hopes to win the war for customers' hearts, minds, and wallets. And this is exactly why it is vital that CX leaders earn influence among their peers, become strategic partners to C-suite executives, and align themselves with the revenue centers that can apply customer data to drive improvement, innovation, and growth.

Step by Step

You'll remember that, in *Chapter 8*, we wrote that eradicating neglect is a prerequisite for transforming customer experience into a revenue driver for your company. And embracing the human cloud is the easiest and most efficient means of eradicating neglect.

It might not surprise you to know that embracing the human cloud is also a prerequisite to stepping into a more strategic role because it frees CX professionals from the time-intensive tasks of forecasting and workforce management. "Partnering with an on-demand network for digital support is key in allowing teams to focus their energies on more strategic initiatives," Jake Lechnir explains. "Rather than spending a lot of management time on staffing and forecasting, CX teams are able to spend more time doing things like looking at support data, getting to the root cause of the issues people reach out about, then working with peers across the organization to use these insights to improve the business."

The way the key components of NOW CX build upon one another is no accident. And this is exactly what we'll explore in *Part 4*. That's where we'll introduce a maturity model that you can use to benchmark your current CX capabilities and map your course toward industry-leading NOW CX success.

PART 4

NOW CX in Practice: Execution Design

CHAPTER 11

Introducing the NOW CX Maturity Model

Netflix Binges on Experience

Contact center work might seem like strange subject matter for a feature film, but this doesn't mean moviemakers haven't found a variety of ways to mine the world of customer service for entertainment. Take, for example, the 2006 comedic thriller *Big Nothing*. David Schwimmer stars as Charlie, an ex-professor turned reluctant call center agent who gets fired on day one of his new job and—desperate for money—gets involved with another disgruntled agent's plot to blackmail a prominent customer using compromising information found in the company's database. If you'd like to check out *Big Nothing* for your next movie night, you won't find it on Netflix. And if you're looking for a real-world example that resembles *Big Nothing*'s unflattering take on contact centers and the people who staff them, you won't find that at Netflix either.

Despite being known today as a driving force in the on-demand economy, many of the video platform's earliest innovations were less about speed than they were about service. By bringing shelf space to the computer screen, dropping DVDs on doorsteps, and making late fees a thing of the past, the company bested Blockbuster's brick-and-mortar rental model. But in early 2007, when Netflix appeared to be stalling in the face of stiffer competition from Blockbuster Online's carbon copy mail order DVD service, it was the startup's commitment to excellent customer service that became its secret weapon.

According to a *New York Times* article from around that time, Netflix doubled down on 24/7, U.S.-based telephone support to "get closer to the customer" while "everyone else is making it almost impossible to find a human."[1] It was a strategy that bucked other companies' efforts to cut back or offshore customer service, and a strategy that stood in stark contrast to Blockbuster, "which outsources a portion of its customer service, and when people do call, they are encouraged to use the Web site instead. Its call center is open only during business hours."[2]

At the same time, Netflix "has tried to give the service representatives more discretion in deciding when to assuage disgruntled callers with bonus discs and account credits—and they are allowed to err on the side of generosity... Netflix places no particular requirements on call duration, preferring that customer service representatives take the time they need to keep a customer happy and loyal... And it is up to the call center representatives to help retain customers."[3]

More than a decade later, the Netflix approach to customer care is more digital, for sure. They offer around-the-clock live chat and use email strategically, although phone is still at the center of their strategy. And the kind of customer centricity Netflix exhibited early-on has become a cornerstone of the company's culture of *customer obsession*.

As described by former Netflix vice president of product, Gibson Biddle, customer obsession ups the ante on mere customer focus in six important ways.[4]

Customer Focus	Customer Obsession
Listen to what customers say	Test and learn via consumer science
Understand customers' current wants and needs	Invent and deliver on unanticipated future needs
Focus on customer satisfaction	Aspire to long-term customer delight
Provide better product than competition	Pioneer new frontiers, with less competition
Balance customer satisfaction and margin, to build a business	Lead with customer delight, ensure work is hard-to-copy, higher margins will follow

While stellar service gave Netflix an edge over Blockbuster in the pre-streaming era, customer *obsession* gives the company its edge in the on-demand economy when thousands upon thousands of entertainment alternatives vie for viewers' attention. As customer experience expert Steven van Belleghem writes on the *CustomerThink* blog, this "has tremendous repercussions on the customer experience as it means that Netflix has to constantly battle for attention in a big red ocean and has no other choice but to offer absolute top-quality experiences and products."[5]

In practice, customer obsession (and the science of using data to understand subscribers better than anyone else) has led Netflix to reinvent its core business model several times over, evolving from a mail order service into a movie streaming platform, and then again into an award-winning content production house. It's what makes the user experience so seamless, personalized, and delightful. It informs the development of bingeworthy original programming like *Tiger King* and *The Queen's Gambit* that, in turn, become levers for increased attention, time spent viewing, and customer loyalty.

And customer obsession keeps Netflix contact center agents on the front lines of relationship management. "It's not just testing, data and algorithms that makes Netflix an absolute king of customer experience," writes Steven van Bellenghem. "They are one of the most human brands as well, with an exceptional customer service. On top of a wide range of self-help solutions in case of problems, English live support is available 24/7... through live chat or via phone. And each of the customer support members is fully trained to focus on joy instead of second guessing the customer."[4]

Beyond all of this, Netflix has built a solid reputation for proactive support, seeking to address and resolve issues without waiting for the customer to call and complain. Let's say you're settling down to binge *Behind Her Eyes* when you notice the sound is out of sync with the picture. Or maybe the video buffers before the streaming even starts. Even if you don't contact support, you might receive an unprompted email in which Netflix owns up to the problem and offers a credit—not because you asked for one, but because it is the right thing to do. It's the kind of experience that costs little, pays huge dividends, and can turn a loyal subscriber into a vocal advocate.

A Model for CX Maturity?

So, is Netflix a model case of customer experience maturity?

The company provides its customers with 24/7/365 human-first support by phone and on at least one key digital channel. Agents are managed for excellence, not efficiency, and use conversations to drive customer loyalty and maximize customer lifetime value. Their interactions are personal, empathetic, proactive, and uniquely human. The entire organization isn't just customer focused; it is customer *obsessed*. And a robust understanding of subscriber needs, wants, and behaviors sits at the heart of strategy, at the core of culture, and is the intelligence behind every data-driven decision the company makes. They embody so many of the outcomes NOW CX sets out to achieve.

But...

Netflix has achieved these outcomes and become a beacon of CX excellence without exhibiting many of the core tenets of NOW CX, as we've defined them. They've been steadfast in maintaining a traditional, phone-first contact center, staffed with hundreds of in-house employees. They haven't adopted a deliberate push toward conversational commerce, although their agents are empowered to exceed customer expectations, which in turn creates loyalty and stems attrition. The company's CX leaders haven't had to sell the value of customer centricity to the C-suite or fight for seats at the strategic table—because they occupied those seats from the very start.

And that's the key distinction between Netflix—or Amazon, Zappos, and other customer experience gamechangers, for that matter—and the average customer service team. Organizations like Netflix were built around CX from the start. They are the companies that other businesses need to catch up with because they are the companies that raised the bar for the NOW Customer.

Could you get to modern CX maturity by the same means used by Netflix? Sure, *in theory.* Are you prepared to turn your internal contact center in a 24/7/365 operation? And staff it with hundreds more agents around the clock, regardless of peaks and dips in demand? But not just *any* agents; high caliber professionals who are natural, creative problem solvers? Even on the overnight shift? And will you measure their performance based on their contribution to loyalty and lifetime value, rather than call volume, handle time or even the blurry measures of customer satisfaction? Can you make all of this happen because you've already convinced your corporate leaders that customer experience deserves to be at the core of the company, at the heart of its strategy, and that insights from your buyer interactions should inform every data-driven decision? You *do* have a seat at the strategic table, right?

Our point isn't that you've gotten these things wrong. It's that you *can* get everything right. But if you're like most CX leaders in most organizations, you're starting from behind because your company was wed to an outdated notion of customer service and an outmoded model for delivering it since well before your first day on the job. So, you will need a new and different toolkit to get to your desired destination.

Naturally, we believe that NOW CX provides that toolkit. And that, applied properly to your customer experience strategy, it will move you toward industry-leading maturity. To see why, let's recap what you've learned so far.

What You've Experienced, So Far

In *Part 1*, we contrasted the old contact center model with a new approach for NOW CX that breaks free of the analog past to bring customer service fully into the digital present and align it with the high expectations of the NOW Customer. We introduced the five shifts that differentiate the latter from the former and we provided you with a clear sense of what the before and after states of customer experience transformation look like.

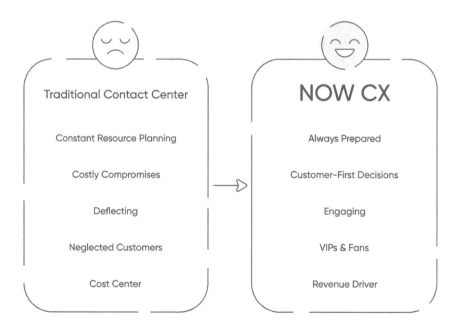

We highlighted the urgent opportunity for modern CX to move beyond the legacy contact center model, and we believe we made a compelling case (financial and otherwise) for overcoming the limitations that model has placed on your brand. At a time when customer experience is at the heart of your brand and CX is one of the last remaining competitive moats, when detractors can inflict pain far beyond their own purchase power and advocates drive both revenue and reputation, when conversations can drive commerce and your CX team can leverage its treasure trove of customer data to inform decisions across the entire company, making the leap to NOW CX provides organizations like yours with a meaningful competitive advantage.

With NOW CX, your customer service operation can serve customers always and across every channel, without arduous preparation or faulty forecasting. Customers truly come first, as you move away from costly, budget-, resource- and efficiency-constrained compromises. You can choose to be more like Netflix or Zappos, actively engaging your customers (with fewer limits) instead of deflecting volume to minimize the cost of care. You make backlogs and wait times a thing of the past, delivering quick responses and high-quality resolutions that make average customers feel like VIPs. And when you have a model that delivers all of this, you create a community of brand fans who buy and buy again. You put your CX team in the driver's seat for direct revenue generation. And you earn a seat at the strategic table.

This is a far cry from run-of-the-mill customer experience, and it requires more than just a new way of thinking about CX. It requires a new way of doing CX. And so, in *Parts 2* and *3*, we laid out a new set of tools and capabilities that mark the journey to NOW CX: the human cloud network, a smarter and more strategic use of technology, conversational commerce, an expanded set of KPIs, and a data-driven approach to customer centricity.

Now, it's time to connect the dots and put you on the path to NOW CX success.

The NOW CX Maturity Model

It's one thing to paint a picture of a better future for customer experience organizations and the people who lead them. It's another thing entirely to provide a practical, step-by-step roadmap. The more we thought about NOW CX as an approach, the more we recognized that CX leaders would need a framework to follow: One that establishes key stages for CX transformation. One that stipulates and sequences the necessary steps. One that provides benchmarks by which CX professionals can measure the progress made by their organization and in their own career.

With all of this in mind, we developed our three-stage *NOW CX Maturity Model:*

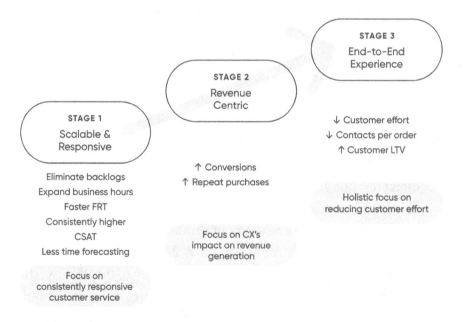

If the legacy contact center model is CX Stage Zero, getting to Stage 1 means making the move toward a scalable staffing model that optimizes your service and support organization to deliver a consistent, responsive, omni-channel experience for every NOW Customer. As a CX leader, you'll spend less time forecasting, reduce workforce management issues, approach "perfect efficiency," gain "spike protection," and achieve consistently higher satisfaction scores. We explored the obstacles and opportunities related to Stage 1 in the second section of this book.

Organizations in Stage 2 have transitioned from cost center to revenue driver. They leverage customer understanding and product expertise to turn pre-sale customer interactions into opportunities to establish brand preference, recommend relevant products, improve conversions, and simplify the buying process. Then, they maintain a connection with the customer to foster upsells, cross-sells, repeat purchases and referrals. The walls that separate CX from marketing, sales, and even ecommerce operations weaken as CX begins to function as a profit center. As a CX leader, you gain the ability to change the perception of CX (and yourself) among your peers and company leadership. In *Chapter 7*, you saw how eradicating neglect lays the foundation and how techniques like conversational commerce allow CX teams to build new revenue generation competencies.

By Stage 3, CX delivers a holistic, whole company—*and whole customer*—experience that reduces customer effort and maximizes lifetime value. A fully mature NOW CX operation is no longer constrained to service and support. Customer obsession drives the entire organization, a robust customer understanding underlies every operational decision, and customer experience is recognized as central to corporate strategy. As the person leading CX at a Stage 3 organization, you are seen as a forward-looking senior executive who has earned a seat at the table alongside top-level decisionmakers in marketing, sales, operations, and finance. In *Chapter 9*, we argued that transitioning CX into a strategic role is both natural and necessary for any organization looking to thrive in the age of the NOW Customer, while in *Chapter 8* we laid out an expanded set of metrics to help you demonstrate that the value of CX extends well beyond mere satisfaction.

We hope that you're as excited as we are about what adopting a mature NOW CX model can mean for you, your team, your company, and even the entire industry.

But...

From Zero to Hero

We have some bad news. And you probably already know what it is: Most CX organizations are stuck at Stage Zero. The odds are that you are too. Fixed and rigid, instead of scalable and flexible. Besieged by backlogs and beholden to business hours. Neglecting shoppers across a range of must-have digital touchpoints as you struggle to be consistently responsive to the demands of your NOW Customers. Never mind driving revenue, spearheading strategy, or delivering a true end-to-end, effortless experience at every stage of the customer lifecycle.

There *is*, of course, good news as well. In reading this book, you have already learned about all the core components of a successful NOW CX strategy. And you've seen how companies like Restaurant Brands International, Happiest Baby, ANINE BING, Shopify, Shutterstock, mmhmm, and others are already incorporating some of these concepts and approaches to break free of the CX status quo. Now, we're about to tie everything together to help you see how you can put all the elements of NOW CX to work in your own organization.

In *Chapter 12*, we'll explain what you'll need to do to get to *Stage 1*, advance to *Stage 2*, then arrive at *Stage 3*. The rubber, as they say, is about to hit the road. And then we'll introduce you to a tool for gauging your own CX maturity and identifying the next steps in your journey toward delivering a best-in-class experience that will win the hearts, minds, and wallets of your most discerning NOW Customers.

CHAPTER 12

The Journey Toward NOW CX Maturity

Say Goodbye to the Status Quo

Customer neglect. At Stage Zero, it's eating away at the very foundation of your business—whether you're aware of it or not. This challenge arises out of the gap between the experience today is demanding, the experience digital consumers expect, and the experience most companies deliver. When organizations narrow (ideally, close) this gap, they do more than just eradicate neglect. They also lay the foundation for a total transformation of the customer service function—repositioning it as a viable and valuable generator of revenue and elevating its stature as a strategic catalyst for customer obsession across the entire business.

In the previous chapter, we introduced our three-stage CX maturity model:

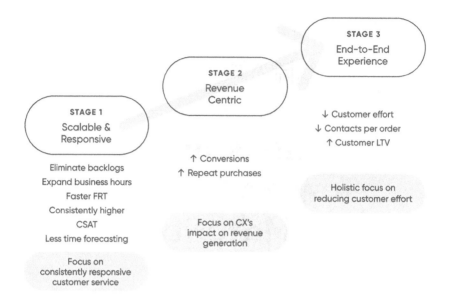

Now, we're going to dig deeper into how your organization can advance through each stage of this model to achieve NOW-era customer experience excellence. We'll describe each step you can take, the key initiatives that will get you there, how the experience you'll deliver stands apart from the status quo, and how you'll measure your success at each stage. As we do this, we'll revisit many of the concepts we've presented throughout the first three sections of this book and, this time around, we'll show how these building blocks fit together to form the basis for customer experience maturity. And finally, we'll look at how two of Simplr's brand partners are turning the components of NOW CX into a formula that delivers a better experience for their customers and better results for their company.

Let's begin with Stage One.

Stage One: Scalable & Responsive CX

CX teams at Stage One eradicate neglect by breaking free from the fixed, rigid contact center model and becoming a scalable, flexible organization that delivers consistently responsive customer service.

Customer service at a Stage One company has three defining characteristics that take direct aim at the two primary reasons NOW Customers feel they've been left hanging—in other words, neglected—by a brand: lack of availability and slow response times. Here's what the three characteristics of a Stage One experience look like:

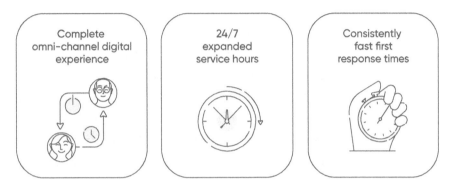

- <u>Complete Omni-Channel Digital Experience</u>. Enable CX across *all* channels, ensuring that every customer can interact through their own preferred methods: chat, email, messaging, social media, phone, or some combination of all these touch points at different times and for different reasons. This alone can be a powerful differentiator given that roughly half of the companies we mystery shopped during the first half of 2021 didn't have chat—a primary channel for NOW Customers overall and Millennial and Generation Z shoppers in particular—enabled at all, and a quarter of those that did didn't have it enabled on their actual ecommerce product pages.[1] Even so, omni-channel presence is just the first of three distinguishing features of a Stage One customer experience. Companies at this level of CX maturity also offer...
- <u>24/7 Expanded Service Hours</u>. Replace regular business hours with around-the-clock support, ensuring that customers have a way to engage with your brand during nightly ecommerce

peaks, weekends, holidays, and any time they're shopping or looking for information. Together, an omni-channel experience and 24/7 service provide the kind of choice, flexibility, and availability NOW Customers expect, while eliminating the backlogs that accumulate when peak volume overwhelms your phone lines or off-hour requests languish in the queue. Which brings us to...

- Consistently Fast First Response Times. Brands that respond to chat and messaging requests in 30 seconds or less and reply to incoming email queries within three hours show that they are attentive to shoppers' needs and committed to rapid resolutions. Consistently meeting the consumer's need for speed—across all channels and especially during off-hours peaks—typically results in higher customer satisfaction ratings and net promoter scores.

As we argued in *Chapters 3* and (especially) *4*, achieving always-on, fast, and flexible customer service is unbearably difficult—if not outright impossible—within the constraints of the legacy contact center model. For this reason, the first stage of NOW CX maturity focuses heavily on rethinking and remaking the customer service staffing model.

Rethink the Human Resources Model

Getting to Stage One means adopting a scalable staffing model that optimizes your service and support organization to deliver a consistent, responsive, omni-channel experience for every NOW Customer. And embracing the human cloud is the smartest and most effective means of eradicating neglect.

As a reminder, future-of-work experts and *The Human Cloud* authors Matthew Mottola and Matthew Coatney wrote that, "The *human cloud* is the platform by which people and businesses can easily and quickly find and work with other people in a digital, remote, and outcome-based way. Consider it the 'office in the cloud,' since it translates everything that happens in a physical office through a digital equivalent."[2] But for customer service in particular, we see the human cloud as just one of three important components of a next generation staffing strategy.

Building on the human cloud's digital-first, highly distributed model for flexible work, we contend that embracing an on-demand expert workforce as part of a three-part, multi-lane CX staffing model is at the core of your opportunity to rethink, then rearchitect your entire human resources model. This is, in fact, the primary work involved in reaching Stage One of NOW CX maturity. So, let's look at how you can approach this shift in your own organization.

*　*　*

Our three-part model proposes an allocation of tickets between human agents (e.g., 80-90% of all volume) and responsibly employed automation (e.g., 10-20% of volume), with a further split among human agents between your internal workforce and a human cloud network of external, on-demand customer service experts. The percentages will be unique to your organization and situation, but our numbers provide a good rule of thumb, and the basic model looks like this:

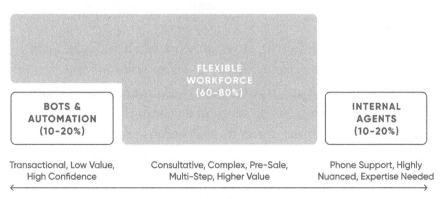

FLEXIBLE
WORKFORCE
(60-80%)

BOTS &
AUTOMATION
(10-20%)

INTERNAL
AGENTS
(10-20%)

Transactional, Low Value,
High Confidence

Consultative, Complex, Pre-Sale,
Multi-Step, Higher Value

Phone Support, Highly
Nuanced, Expertise Needed

FULL SPAN OF TICKETS

Let's work through this model, right to left, beginning with your internal agents.

Elevate Your Internal Agents

In the multi-lane model, internal agents—your most expensive resource—are best reserved for solving your customers' most sophisticated challenges. With your internal agents focused on the highest value customer interactions and other strategic CX priorities, a human cloud network of on-demand agents takes a leading role in handling a substantial majority of your volume, addressing peak demand, and filling any gaps in your 24/7 omni-channel strategy.

Activate an On-Demand (Human Cloud) Workforce

Qualified freelance agents—employed on-demand in a human cloud network—can handle any inquiries that exceed the capacity of your automated options but don't rise to the standard you set for high touch internal agents. The volume you direct (not defer!) to a flexible workforce might include the bulk of your customers' routine requests, but you don't need to draw the line there. With access to the right tools and information, on-demand agents can also tackle complex matters, use consultative approaches in both pre- and post-sale situations, engage in multi-step customer service processes, and handle higher value interactions that you would not entrust to a chatbot.

Done right, your human cloud network can handle the majority of your customer service requests—at scale, without arduous training, with a level of "perfect efficiency" that dynamically scales up *and down* to match peaks and lulls in demand, all without the need for an inherently faulty forecast. And because the human cloud is digital-by-definition, these workers are uniquely suited to handle most (or even all) of the digital touchpoints preferred by many NOW Customers for their ease and immediacy: email, chat, messaging, and even social customer service.

Now, let's turn our attention to the third part of the multi-lane CX staffing model: chatbots, automation, and self-service.

Set Up Your Chatbots for Success

In *Chapter 5*, we weighed the pros and cons of chatbots for customer service, cautioning brands against over-indexing on automation. That said, we did advocate a reasonable, responsible approach to integrating bots into a human-first, technology-enabled model for delivering NOW CX. As we wrote:

> In practice, this means relying on automation alone only when you feel 100% confident that the technology can provide a satisfactory resolution and reduce the amount of effort required on the part of the customer. And it means that wherever and whenever chatbots or other forms of automation are at work, you're also providing your customers with access to—and a quick, seamless handoff to—human agents if and when they need it. If your company offers 24/7/365 chatbot support, your customers expect 24/7/365 human support. It really is that simple. And for any conversation that is complex, complicated, high-value, high stakes, or consultative in nature, you'd be wise to opt for human-first engagement. Otherwise, the cost savings of automation likely aren't worth the potential lost revenue or the high cost of customer neglect.

This perspective informed our three-part framework for multi-lane NOW CX. And it should guide your approach to automation as you build out your hybrid model for staffing an efficient and effective 24/7 omni-channel operation.

Integrate bots (and other forms of automation) in ways that contribute to your efforts to eradicate customer neglect without diminishing the benefits of your human-first focus. In practice, this means setting realistic expectations for how well technology can serve consumers, investing in well-designed decision trees and adequate training of the algorithms, and keeping a human "in the loop" at all times to ensure seamless and effective hand-offs whenever tech-only interactions can't meet the customer's needs.

Once you have the pieces in place, be sure to measure the performance of your hybrid engagements, identify gaps, and continually improve the quality of the service, hand-offs, and resolutions. And this brings us to the matter of measuring whether your Stage One efforts are paying off.

Measuring Stage One Success

Brands that reach Stage One can measure their effectiveness by tracking improvements across several core customer service metrics: faster first response times, improved efficiency, and higher CSAT and Net Promoter scores. At the same time, CX leaders will find themselves spending significantly less time forecasting and agents will experience more job satisfaction, lower stress, and higher engagement as the multi-lane model frees them to focus on higher priority tickets and more rewarding CX projects.

As you make both the legacy contact center model and customer neglect relics of the past, you prepare your organization to take its next step toward CX maturity—and set the stage for the work necessary to reach Stage Two.

Stage Two: The Revenue-Centric CX Organization

CX teams at Stage Two move beyond stemming the losses that accrue because of customer neglect. They empower agents to identify and act upon more opportunities to drive revenue by engaging buyers in personalized, contextually relevant conversations that result in higher conversions, more cross-selling, and larger order sizes. In doing so, CX escapes the cost center stigma that forces customer service leaders to make so many costly compromises.

The three defining characteristics of customer service at a Stage Two company take their flexible, scalable, and responsive multi-lane organization to the next level by turning it into an engine for business growth. Stage Two CX is defined by the following three attributes:

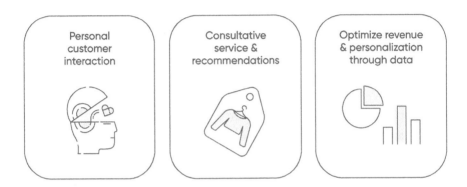

- <u>Personalized Customer Interaction</u>. Fostering meaningful one-on-one connections between agents and customers allows brands to be more human and builds relationships that lead to loyalty over time. This approach calls for brands to put data and customer understanding to use, and directly into the hands of frontline service personnel. Armed with this data, your agents can facilitate customer service interactions that reference past shopping experiences and purchases, make proactive recommendations based on behavior, and even build rapport and deepen relationships by referencing relevant life stages, local news, or world events.
- <u>Consultative Service & Recommendations</u>. Enable your agents to serve as consultants to your customers, helping them buy with confidence and ease. Harness historical data, past and present shopping behavior, and information gleaned through real-time interactions to offer well-honed product recommendations whenever a customer engages an agent through any service channel. Use each conversation as an opportunity

to help the customer buy, and each interaction as a way to drive conversions, cross-sell and upsell additional products, stimulate repurchase, and maximize average order size.

- Optimize Revenue & Personalization Through Data: Data can do more than just improve individual interactions. When collected across the board and analyzed at a macro level, data can provide valuable insights into what is or isn't working on the whole when it comes to delighting your customers and translating CX into incremental revenue. Put analytics to work by optimizing every key component of your CX program—from agent performance and chatbot interactions to site structure and ecommerce purchase path—and stripping away any hurdle that stands in the way of turning your customer service team into a revenue driving force for your company.

While *Chapter 8* presented a couple of ways for companies to generate revenue through customer experience, conversational commerce is the most immediate and actionable way for most CX teams to generate incremental business. For this reason, launching and scaling a conversational commerce capability within your CX organization should be the primary focus of Stage Two maturity.

Connect Conversations to Commerce

In *Chapter 8*, we explained that conversational commerce leverages the power of dialogue to offer a personalized, consultative shopping experience that ultimately drives sales and revenue. Customer service messaging is a critical component of conversational commerce in the digital environment because it allows your human specialists to replicate the one-on-one, in-store salesperson experience by enabling them to interact with customers in real-time during the buying process, provide in-the-moment help, and offer relevant recommendations while fostering relationships.

Conversational commerce requires traditional customer service leaders to rethink the way they handled messaging before they began their journey to NOW CX—making shifts from bot-first to human-first, from tactical to strategic, and from transactional to truly conversational. You already set the stage for this by adopting a flexible, scalable multi-lane staffing model; now you'll expand the focus of that human-first, technology-enabled operation to go beyond providing information and resolving issues. Conversations will become an avenue for delivering personalized services and product recommendations; a means of reducing customer effort by making interactions with your brand simple, helpful, and useful; and a driver of incremental revenue that can be attributed directly to your CX team.

In a nutshell, conversational commerce turns every CX specialist into an online personal shopping assistant who knows how to turn each customer service interaction into an opportunity to add value for the buyer while capturing value for the company in the form of increased average order size. In practice, this means equipping your agents with the ability to make relevant upsell recommendations, suggest complementary products, provide alternative options when preferred items are out of stock, and turning returns into exchanges.

Technology Provides Instant Access to Information

For conversational commerce to work in practice, any agent tasked with commerce in their conversations must have access to the just-in-time information they'll need, in a simple user-friendly platform that ties directly into your customer data repository, ecommerce platform, inventory management system, shopping cart software, ticketing, and other customer support systems. This system should proactively present the agent with contextually relevant personal and commercial "connection prompts" that will allow them to naturally move any given conversation toward easier engagement and a more satisfying and profitable purchasing experience. These just-in-time prompts will allow the agent to build rapport, ask the right questions, provide relevant information, offer knowledgeable recommendations, and highlight promotions, offers, and incentives that increase the likelihood of purchase.

Finally, when these capabilities are provided via cloud-based technology to both internal employees and external on-demand agents, you equip all members of your hybrid service and support team to be effective revenue-focused consultants to your customers.

Measuring Stage Two Success

If Stage One is measured by improvements to core metrics like speed, efficiency, and customer satisfaction, success in Stage Two is gauged by your CX team's ability to generate incremental revenue consistently, reliably, and professionally. Metrics like average order size and repeat purchase rate demonstrate your organization's ability to drive measurable business outcomes. Proving that great CX provides the company with an additional path to profit helps ensure that senior leadership takes you seriously and sets the stage for turning your customer service organization into a key source of strategic business value.

And this brings us to Stage Three.

Stage Three: A Strategic Seat at the Table

With a flexible and responsive workforce in place and a working model for revenue generation in action, CX is ready to take the ultimate step: to transform the nature of experience you deliver so fundamentally and fully that it sets your company apart from your competitors and cements your role as a strategic asset far beyond the boundaries of the customer service department.

For your customers, Stage Three delivers a wholistic, end-to-end experience that minimizes their effort in three important ways.

Lowest effort path to every inquiry

Seamless handoffs from bot to human

Proactive issue avoidance

- <u>Lowest Effort Path to Every Inquiry</u>. Offer each customer the fastest and most convenient way to get the information they need, when they need it, through their preferred channel of choice. To deliver this, brands might leverage automation for its speed, particularly at the first touch in digital service channels, provided that technology is capable of delivering accurate and appropriate responses and that there is always a human-first on-ramp when needed.
- <u>Seamless Handoffs from Bot to Human</u>. As we've already argued, automation alone is likely to fall short of consumer expectations and isn't well-suited to the nuanced nature of commerce-oriented conversations. For these reasons, it's vital that brands ensure that there is always a human in-the-loop, that escalations happen quickly (within seconds), that the agent has the full context of the prior interaction between the customer and the bot, and that the agent is equipped (they have the necessary information) and empowered (they have permission) to solve the customer's problem.
- <u>Proactive Issue Avoidance</u>. Most of all though, Stage Three NOW CX is characterized by a proactive stance toward issue resolution. Using data, identify and operationalize fixes to

common causes of customer service cases, points of friction at the point of purchase and across the customer lifecycle, and any remaining risks that could result in customer neglect. In a nutshell, avoid issues before they happen by addressing them before customers are even aware the issues exist.

At the same time, Stage Three calls for and results in a fundamentally different role (and stature) for CX inside the organization. One that truly—and perhaps for the first time in many companies—grants customer-facing leadership a seat at the table. Getting to this stage means delivering on three important opportunities for CX beyond the service center.

Become a Strategic Partner to the C-Suite

Whether your company has a chief experience officer, you *are* the chief experience officer, or you've yet to put a senior customer service leader in the C-suite, one thing is clear: in an age when customer experience is the last remaining competitive moat, every company needs customer champions. And as we argued in *Chapter 10*, there are no better champions for the customer than the people who are on the front lines, interacting with that customer every day. *You*. Further, the fact that siloed CX projects may be scattered across the organization calls for a strong leader who can integrate these disparate efforts into the unified end-to-end experience Stage Three companies deliver. *Also, you.*

By stepping into both roles, CX professionals become a strategic partner to senior leaders and peers, drive an increased sense of customer-centricity that infuses CX-related projects (wherever they're managed in the company), and ultimately shape strategic decisions made everywhere in the organization.

On one level, influence is a function of the strong, mutually beneficial relationships you build with executives in other parts of the business. On another, influence is earned by the level of customer and CX subject matter expertise you bring to those relationships—and your ability to shape the way your peers and leaders in your organization think about and serve the customer.

Achieve Tighter Alignment with (Other) Revenue-Driving Teams

As we explored in *Chapter 10*, it's also essential that CX aligns more closely with other revenue-oriented parts of the organization, including sales, customer success, ecommerce, and (maybe even especially) marketing. Note that there is no one "right" way to make this happen. In some companies, this might literally mean combining the two functions into a single department reporting to one senior executive. In others, a cross-departmental taskforce might prove more effective.

Regardless of your chosen structure, several constants are clear: a common culture, shared mindset, and even aligned business objectives and goals will lay the groundwork for a more integrated, effective, and strategic approach to the customer that the whole company can buy into.

Empower Customer-Informed Decisions Everywhere in the Organization

Finally, the most customer-obsessed brands put customer data and insights at the center of their decisions—not just about customer experience, but about products, services, innovation, operations, and more. In fact, the more important customer insights become to the business overall—and the better the customer service team becomes at capturing and channeling those insights to the people who can use them for strategic decision-making—the more central CX becomes to the company.

For starters—and an essential element of Stage Three CX maturity—customer complaints often illuminate more widespread issues that the company can address proactively and preemptively before they impact a larger portion of its customer base. We call this *proactive issue avoidance*: solving challenges even before your customers know they exist by identifying and operationalizing fixes to the underlying causes of buyer friction, customer complaints, and even neglect.

Beyond this, the strategic application of customer insights beyond CX creates a scenario in which the voice of the customer ultimately factors into a wide array of product and service decisions. In short, Stage Three organizations don't act on *anything* until they understand the implications for the customer.

Measuring Stage Three Success

Stage Two already introduced financial metrics into the mix. In Stage Three, you'll take this even further by focusing on how excellent CX increases not only average order size but lifetime customer value. At the same time, where Stage One sought to eradicate neglect, Stage Three—through its emphasis on providing a holistic and consistent end-to-end experience—aims to minimize customer effort.

*   *   *

Before we guide you even further down the path toward your own CX transformation, let's look at the impact some of these steps are having in two real companies.

Seeing NOW CX in Practice

At Simplr, we have plenty of experience helping companies break free of Stage Zero customer support and make the move into NOW CX. It's what we do. And while we don't want to dilute the broader message of this book, we do think it's worth looking at how just a couple of the real companies we serve are revolutionizing their service model and achieving results that are only possible with a truly scalable, revenue-centric NOW CX model.

Princess Polly

Online fashion boutique Princess Polly might have been born in an Australian beachside apartment, but today the company boasts a global brand with trend-conscious customers around the world. After struggling with surges in tickets, email overloads, and jammed phone lines—especially outside of normal Aussie business hours— director of operations Alexandria Collis took an important step toward NOW CX. Princess Polly introduced 24/7 live chat, staffed by a blended team of internal agents and Simplr's human cloud network of on-demand specialists.

As a result, Alexandria's service organization—a meshed team of internal agents and Simplr experts—connects with more Princess Polly customers faster, responding to 90% of all chats in under 30 seconds. At the same time, the company has seen a 46% reduction in costly phone volume, is running at a higher level of efficiency overall, and has happier in-house agents. "24/7 chat coverage really helps our team to stay productive and it helps our company's culture," Alexandria shared. "[Our] agents feel good at work knowing that they're not as stressed or having to deal with 'low-hanging fruit' questions."[3]

Just as important, speed, around-the-clock availability, and employee engagement are really starting to pay off at Princess Polly. The brand sees a 17% conversion rate on agent-assisted purchases, and the customers who engage with customer service are 42% more likely to buy again than those who don't.[4] Pre-sale messaging and best-in-class CX enables the brand to meet the NOW Customer in-the-moment and forge a link between customer service and revenue growth—a clear measure of Stage Two NOW CX performance and a strong basis for making customer service a strategic strength for the business overall.

Mack Weldon

Menswear brand Mack Weldon has seen similar success with human cloud-powered 24/7 chat. Counting on outside agents who—thanks to the use of enabling technology—ramp quickly, require little to no onboarding, and still provide the same high quality the company expects of its own employees, Mack Weldon averages a 23-minute first response time over email and a mere 12 seconds over chat. Performance like this, delivered around the clock, has helped the brand achieve an average CSAT score of 4.84/5 across all tickets.[5]

At the same time, Mack Weldon taps into conversational commerce to mirror the brand's in-store experience and convert more customers. Simplr's conversational commerce capabilities use artificial intelligence to enable all Simplr Specialists to make personalized product recommendations based on a customer's inquiry or their past purchase history. "When buyers on our site have questions about our products, we really want to mirror those engagements that they would get in a store—letting customers have real conversations with us and making buying easier," explains customer service manager Pat Feehan. "Our goal isn't to act as salespeople. Being able to recommend products they might like based on what they're asking about or what they've bought from us before often adds a lot of value to the experience."

By embracing Stage Two conversational commerce, Mack Weldon has escaped the cost center stigma and is proving its value as a contributor to revenue growth. Today, the brand converts 28% of its pre-sale conversations into purchases—an eight-point lift over conversion rates before introducing conversational commerce capabilities.[6]

As Mack Weldon's CX team prepares to step further into the strategic center of the business, they are using data and revenue insights to highlight and demonstrate how their commitment to providing exceptional service is truly impacting the business beyond typical operational service metrics. Feehan says, "Being able to report out on how our engagement strategy can drive revenue, and how we help the bottom line, is a huge win. It's great for us to be recognized for things other than CSAT." With the credibility, visibility, and accountability gained through a revenue-centric approach, customer service is now seen as one of three main areas for investment—alongside traditional revenue drivers like marketing and an expanded retail footprint—as the company works to elevate its stature as one of the world's premier brands in the men's basics category.

And NOW, It's Your Turn

The best part of this is that any customer service team can achieve these kinds of results and have this kind of business impact—*including yours*. To help you get started, we're going to introduce you to a tool that will help you gauge where your own CX stands today, understand your own level of NOW CX-readiness, and identify the first (or next) steps you can take to become the kind of organization that wins the hearts, minds, and wallets of today's most demanding NOW Customers.

CHAPTER 13

Welcome to the NOW CX Movement

Start Here!

If you're the kind of person who immediately flips to the back of the book to get straight to the bottom line, these might be the first words you read. So, let us give you an idea of what you've missed—and what's in store for you as you turn back to page one and start over at the beginning. Over the course of a couple hundred pages, we've shared just about everything we know (as of this writing, at least) about the NOW Customer and why so many organizations fail to meet their demand for efficient, empathetic, and effective always-on service. We've also shared how true CX leaders can meet (even exceed) their expectations while creating the future of customer experience by embracing a flexible, scalable, on-demand staffing model, becoming a revenue-centric service organization and elevating CX into the strategic center of the business.

And for those of you who have arrived here at lucky *Chapter 13* after reading this book in a more traditional manner—from front to back—*congratulations*! You've already learned all the key strategies, approaches, tools, and tactics you'll need to join us in building the NOW CX movement. There's just one more thing you'll need to do before you get started: see where your current CX sits on the maturity curve.

CX For Yourself

As a companion to this book, we've developed an online, interactive self-assessment that allows you to gauge exactly where your own customer service organization stands relative to the three stages of NOW CX maturity and—based on your results—guides you toward the first steps you can take on your NOW CX journey. But before you dive into the assessment itself, we'd recommend that you gather some information about your current CX capabilities. Even better, gather the key members of your customer service team and do the work together.

You'll be gauging your current maturity level based on your honest answers to the following 17 questions. Here we go:

1. What metrics are you currently using to measure the success of your customer service department? (Make a list of all that apply.)

2. For each of the metrics you just listed, what is your current level of performance for each of the metrics you use today?

3. On which channels is real-time support offered? (List them all.)

4. What is your average first response time via email?

5. What is your average first response time via chat?

6. How often is your support team staffed? In other words, how many hours per day, which hours each day, and what days (including weekends and holidays) do you provide access to human agents?

7. On which pages of your website do you offer live chat functionality? (List them all.)

8. Is your chatbot enabled with capabilities that allow for empathetic or personalized interactions? For example, can it reference past purchases or support interactions, or can it proactively bring up important personal, local, or global events impacting the customer?

9. Is your support staff trained to have empathetic/personalized conversations with customers that include the same kinds of relevant topics?

10. Are personalized product recommendations for upsell/cross sell purposes something that your chat program provides for customers?

11. How many steps does it take for an average customer service interaction to be resolved? (A 'step' is any time the customer needs to input more information to the bot/agent.)

12. How long, on average, does it take for a chat inquiry to be picked up by a human agent after it has been elevated from a self-service capability?

13. When an inquiry is escalated from self-service to a human, what information does the customer need to repeat to help the human agent 'catch up' with the issue and interaction?

14. Does your CX program proactively engage with customers to provide information or solutions before they reach out to you?

15. Which other functions within your company are actively leveraging data from CX to improve their programs? For example: ecommerce, sales, marketing, corporate strategy, production, finance, the C-suite, or any other department?

16. How strongly do you agree or disagree with this statement: *"My organization values our CX program as being an essential strategic driver of the business and is fundamental to informing the overall direction of the company."*

17. How strongly do you agree or disagree with this statement: *"CX is a revenue driving function at my company."*

OK. Now...

Fire up your browser and navigate to **https://now.simplr.ai/maturity_assessment.** Or grab your smartphone and snap this QR code:

You'll need to register and, when you're done with the survey, check your email for your results and some guidance on your best next steps. *Good luck!* But as you go, don't feel like you'll need to go it alone.

What's Next for You?

We're as curious as you are to see where you stand today. And we're as committed as you are to making sure your company is doing everything it can do to win customers' hearts, minds, and wallets in the era of NOW CX—in the era when experience truly *is* everything.

So, let's build this movement together. Connect with us to discuss your NOW CX maturity scores, get even more ideas for making the movement real inside your own organization, or learn how Simplr can help you eradicate neglect, drive more revenue, and accelerate your progress toward *Stage Three*. Here are some great ways to keep on top of our latest thinking, eye-opening research, and real customer success stories:

- Visit us at www.simplr.ai
- Connect with us at linkedin.com/company/simplr
- Follow us @simplr on Twitter
- And connect directly with both of us. Our info is in our bios at the back of this book.

Welcome to the NOW CX movement. Your next wave of customers is on their way to your site as we speak. They know what they want from your company. When it comes to customer experience (to paraphrase the timeless *and timely* words of the late Freddie Mercury of Queen) *they want it all. And they want it NOW*.

And the good news is: You're ready.

ENDNOTES

Chapter 1

1. "The Great French Wine Blight," *Wine Tidings No. 96*, July/August 1986
2. Chris Simms, "The Grapes of Wrath," *New Scientist*, December 19, 2017
3. Greg Verdino, *microMARKETING: Get Big Results by Thinking and Acting Small*, McGraw-Hill, 2010
4. *State of the Connected Consumer, Fourth Edition*, Salesforce.com, 2021
5. Ibid.
6. Ibid.
7. *State of Online Customer Service*, Simplr Inc., July 2020
8. *State of the Connected Consumer, Fourth Edition*, Salesforce.com, 2021
9. *Leveraging the Value of Emotional Connection for Retailers*, Motista, September 2018
10. *State of the Connected Consumer, Fourth Edition*, Salesforce.com, 2021
11. *Simplr Consumer Online Shopping and Customer Service Study*, Simplr Inc., December 2020
12. *The Future Shopper Report 2020*, Wunderman Thompson Commerce, May 2020
13. *Simplr Consumer Online Shopping and Customer Service Study*, Simplr Inc., December 2020
14. "Keeping Your Customer Service Personal Amid Historic Change," Execs in the Know, September 19, 2020
15. *American Express Global Customer Service Barometer*, American Express, 2017

Chapter 2

1. *Serial Switchers*, NewVoiceMedia, May 2018
2. *MarketWatch*, "Peloton sales triple as pandemic surge continues, but the stock is falling as supply issues worsen," November 2020
3. Ibid.
4. *The New York Times*, "Peloton's Rapid Rise Is Threatened by Its Slow Delivery," January 2021
5. The Verge, "Peloton is spending millions to fix its months-long shipping delays," February 2021
6. PelotonForum.com
7. *The New York Times*, "Peloton's Rapid Rise Is Threatened by Its Slow Delivery," January 2021
8. The Verge, "Peloton is spending millions to fix its months-long shipping delays," February 2021
9. "An Update on Your Delivery Experience," Peloton | The Output, February 2021
10. *The Wall Street Journal*, "Peloton Taps Brakes to Fix Delivery Woes," February 2021
11. Freight Waves, "Peloton's supply chain is broken (and $100m won't fix it)," February 2021
12. Trends 2016: The Future of Customer Service, Forrester, January 2016
13. *Know thy customer: Critical factors impacting customer lifetime value*, Zendesk, December 2018
14. *Simplr Consumer Online Shopping and Customer Service Study*, December 2020
15. *The State of CX and Customer Neglect*, Simplr, January 2021

Chapter 3

Nothing to see here, folks.

Chapter 4

1. John D. Sterman, "Teaching Takes Off," *OR/MS Today*, October 1992
2. ContactBabel, *The US Contact Center Decision-Makers' Guide, 2018-2019*, October 2018
3. YourMatter.com, "The Gig Economy—What Is It? Definition, Examples and Future," February 10, 2020

4. ContactBabel, *The US Contact Center Decision-Makers' Guide, 2018-2019*, October 2018

5. Intuit and Emergent Research, *Dispatches from the New Economy: The On-Demand Economy Worker Study*, June 2017

6. Bureau of Labor Statistics, U.S. Department of Labor, *Contingent and Alternative Employment Arrangements—May 2017*, June 2018

Chapter 5

1. E. Epstein and W.D. Klinkenberg, "From Eliza to Internet: A brief history of computerized assessment." *Computers in Human Behavior*, Volume 17, Issue 3, May 2001

2. Karen Hao, "This Could Lead to the Next Big Breakthrough in Common Sense AI." MIT Technology Review, November 6, 2020

3. V. Pradha and L. Joseph, *How to Scale Your Chatbot*, Forrester Research, December 2019

4. Ibid.

5. Gartner, Inc., *Does Your Digital Customer Service Strategy Deliver?*, September 2019

6. Forrester, K. Cardona Smits et al, *Human Customer Service: The Overlooked Opportunity for Breakaway CX Differentiation*, January 2020

Chapter 6

1. Bruce Temkin and Aimee Lucas, *Employee Engagement Benchmark Study*, Qualtrics XM Institute, March 2017

2. Jacob Morgan, *The Employee Experience Advantage: How to Win the War for Talent by Giving Employees the Workspaces they Want, the Tools they Need, and a Culture They Can Celebrate*, Wiley, 2017

3. Laurie Ruettimann, "The best CX Starts with Making Life Better for Employees," The Future of Customer Engagement and Experience, April 13, 2021

4. Ibid.

5. Blake Morgan, "The Un-Ignorable Link Between Employee Experience and Customer Experience," Forbes.com, February 23, 2018

6. Tina Brown, "The Gig Economy," The Daily Beast, January 12, 2009

7. Matthew Mottola, "What Is the $1.2 Trillion Freelance Economy?," Forbes.com, May 19, 2021

8. Matthew Mottola and Matthew Coatney, *The Human Cloud: How Today's Changemakers Use Artificial Intelligence and the Freelance Economy to Transform Work*, HarperCollins Leadership, 2021

9. Ibid.

10. Upwork.com and the Freelancers Union, *Freelancing in America: 2017*, October 2017

11. Daisuke Wakabayashi, "Google's Shadow Work Force: Temps Who Outnumber Full-Time Employees," New York Times, May 28, 2019

12. Joseph Fuller et al, "Rethinking the On-Demand Workforce," Harvard Business Review, Nov-Dec 2020

13. Didier Bonnet and George Westerman, "The New Elements of Digital Transformation," MIT Sloan Management Review, November 19, 2020

14. Intuit, Emergent Research, *Dispatches from the New Economy: The On-Demand Economy Worker Study*, 2017

15. Microsoft, *2021 Work Trend Index: Annual Report. The Next Great Disruption is Hybrid Work—Are We Ready?*, Match 22, 2021

16. Erica Pandey, "Great Resignation Wave Coming for Companies," Axios.com, June 14. 2021

16. Paul Gillin, "The Gig Economy is a Two-Way Street," ComputerWorld, May 28, 2021

Chapter 7

1. Nicole France, "The Gig Economy Comes to Customer Service," ConstellationR.com, December 9, 2020
2. Zappos.com, "10 Things to Know About Zappos Customer Service," April 17, 2020
3. Zappos.com, "This Phone Rep Bonded with a Customer for 10 Hours," September 18, 2018
4. Nicole France, "The Gig Economy Comes to Customer Service," ConstellationR.com, December 9, 2020

Chapter 8

1. Simplr.ai/after-hours-support
2. *The State of CX and Customer Neglect*, Simplr, January 2021
3. Fred Reichheld, *Prescription for Cutting Costs*, Bain & Company, October 25, 2021
4. Aberdeen Group, *Omni-Channel Customer Care: Empowered Customers Demand a Seamless Experience*, October 2013
5. Forrester, Kate Leggett et al, *Transform the Contact Center for Customer Service Excellence*, January 2021
6. Chris Messina, "Conversation Commerce: Messaging apps bring the point of sale to you," January 15, 2015
7. Susanna Kim, "Comcast Apologizes for 'Unacceptable' Customer Service Call That Won't End, ABCnews.com, July 15, 2014
8. *The State of Conversational Commerce 2021*, Simplr, June 2021
9. Ibid.
10. Ibid.
11. Thomas Lee, "Best Buy is Staking a Big Part of Its Future on Geek Squad," Minneapolis Star Tribune, July 29, 2012
12. Ibid.
13. Ibid.
14. Anthony Dukes and Yi Zhu, "Why is Customer Service So Bad? Because It's Profitable," Harvard Business Review, February 28, 2019

Chapter 9

1. Gartner, "Drive Customer Loyalty and Retention Through Service" August 2020
2. Gartner, "A Better Way for Service to Predict Future Customer Loyalty" November 2020

Chapter 10

1. Andrew Schwager and Chris Meyer, "Understanding Customer Experience," Harvard Business Review, February 2007
2. Tom McCall, "Gartner Predicts a Customer Experience Battlefield," Gartner.com, February 18, 2015
3. Gartner, Inc., *2019 Customer Experience Management Study*, February 2020
4. Andrew Schwager and Chris Meyer, "Understanding Customer Experience," Harvard Business Review, February 2007
5. MarketPro, Inc., "The Master of the Customer Experience: What You Need to Know About the CXO," February 2015
6. Ibid.
7. Kelsey Miller, "How to Influence Without Authority in the Workplace," Harvard Business School Online, October 24, 2019
8. Forrester, *The Future of Customer Insights Will Power Next Best Experiences*, February 2021

[9.] Gartner, Inc. "Gartner Says Nearly 90% of Organizations Now Have a Chief Experience Officer or Chief Customer Officer or Equivalents," February 10, 2020

[10.] Robert Half, "Hot Job: Chief Experience Officer," July 9, 2019

[11.] Forrester., *The State of Customer Analytics 2020*, March 2021

[12.] Forrester, *The Future of Customer Insights Will Power Next Best Experiences*, February 2021

[13.] Ibid.

Chapter 11

[1.] Katie Hafner, "At Netflix, Victory for Voices Over Keystrokes," New York Times, August 16, 2007

[2.] Ibid.

[3.] Ibid.

[4.] Gibson Biddle, "How Netflix's Customer Obsession Created a Customer Obsession," Medium, April 17, 2018

[5.] Steven van Belleghem, "What Can We Learn from Netflix About CX?," CustomerThink.com, January 5, 2021

Chapter 12

[1.] *The State of Conversational Commerce 2021*, Simplr, June 2021

[2.] Matthew Mottola and Matthew Coatney, *The Human Cloud: How Today's Changemakers Use Artificial Intelligence and the Freelance Economy to Transform Work*, HarperCollins Leadership, 2021

[3.] Simplr.ai, "Princess Polly Reduces Phone Volume by 46% with Simplr's 24/7 Live Chat Staffing"

[4.] Ibid.

[5.] Simplr.ai, "Mack Weldon Partners with Simplr to Scale Customer Service, Convert New Customers, and Support Accelerated Growth"

[6.] Ibid.

ABOUT THE AUTHORS

ENG TAN is CEO of Simplr, a company that is redefining the way brands deliver CX. Prior to starting Simplr, he was at Asurion, the largest global consumer tech care company, and Booz Allen Hamilton as an operations and strategy advisor to the Fortune 500. Eng resides in Boston.

You can reach him at
eng@simplr.ai
or at
linkedin.com/in/eng-tan.

DANIEL RODRIGUEZ is an experienced marketing executive, entrepreneur, family guy and musician who uses daily meditation to manage life's intense moments. He currently is the CMO at Simplr, where he's leading a team that is redefining the way brands deliver customer service. Before Simplr, he served as VP of Marketing for Seismic. A native of Cleveland, he's been a Bostonian since earning a BA from Harvard and an MBA from the MIT Sloan School of Management.

Email him at
daniel@simplr.ai
or find him at
LinkedIn.com/in/drodriguez4.

ABOUT SIMPLR

Simplr is the conversational experience platform for the NOW CX era. The company's platform combines automation with AI-powered human assistance to deliver instantly scalable premium pre-sale shopping assistance and customer support. The result for Simplr customers is best-in-class experiences throughout the consumer journey, increasing loyalty, satisfaction, and revenue. Simplr is funded by Asurion, which continues to support its growth.

Learn more at
www.simplr.ai.

CPSIA information can be obtained
at www.ICGtesting.com
Printed in the USA
BVHW030039040822
643657BV00007B/7/J